W9-BMU-857

Making
Designer

SEED BEAD, STONE,
& CRYSTAL JEWELRY

QUARRY

H

Making Designer SEED BEAD, STONE, & CRYSTAL JEWELRY

Tammy Powley

GLOUCESTER MASSACHUSETTS

QUARRY BOOKS

First published in the United States of America by

Quarry Books, a member of
Quayside Publishing Group
33 Commercial Street
Gloucester, Massachusetts 01930-5089
Telephone: (978) 282-9590
Fax: (978) 283-2742
www.rockpub.com

Library of Congress Cataloging-in-Publication Data
Powley, Tammy.
    Making designer seed bead, stone, and crystal jewelry / Tammy Powley.
        p.   cm.
    ISBN 1-59253-245-4 (pbk.)
    1. Beadwork. 2. Jewelry making.   I. Title.
TT860.P697 2006
745.594'2—dc22

2005030269
CIP

ISBN 1-59253-245-4

10 9 8 7 6 5 4 3 2

Design: Dutton & Sherman Design
Photography: Allan Penn
Illustrations: Judy Love

CONTENTS

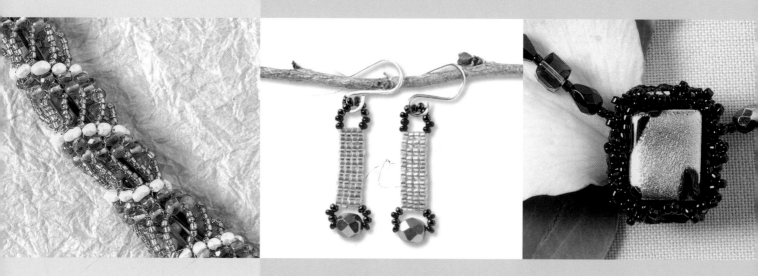

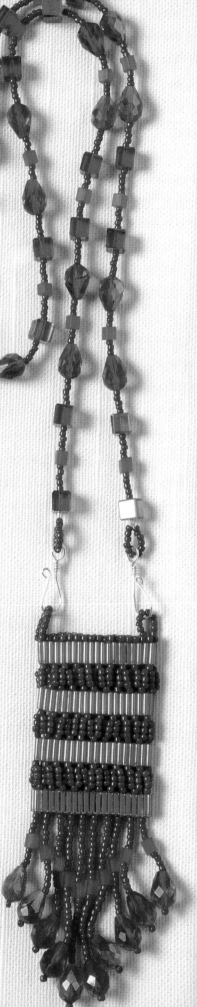

INTRODUCTION

At first, the idea of making seed bead jewelry may seem a little daunting. Those beads are so tiny! But ask any bead weaver and she (or he) will tell you how relaxing it is to sit and stitch beads together to form an infinite assortment of designs. There is truly something magical about these little glass beads. As you weave them together, time slips away, and so do all the stress and worry of the day.

When you enter into the fold of bead weavers, you become part of a tradition that dates back centuries and reaches across the planet. The ancient Egyptians were one of the first cultures to make glass beads. They prized glass as much as precious metal and gems, going so far as to create glass beads resembling gemstones. Glass bead making seemed to languish after this period in history, but this changed around the year 1200, when glass artisans in Italy revived the popularity of glass making. This ignited a thriving glass-producing industry, which included glass beads. Murano, Italy, is still considered the glass capital of the world. By the eighteenth century, new technology allowed factories to overtake the smaller producers, and this opened up the market. The Czech Republic and Japan took advantage of this opportunity and are now two of the largest glass seed bead producers in the world.

One reason glass bead making became such a large industry is because beads were not used primarily for ornamentation, as they usually are today. Rather, beads were a type of currency for travelers. This practice spread glass beads to areas of Africa, the Americas, and the South Pacific.

Explorers traded beads in exchange for food, water, and other daily necessities.

Today, bead weavers from an assortment of cultures and backgrounds continue the tradition of working with glass beads, using them to create jewelry, enhance clothing, or construct home decor items. Among the most popular seed bead pastimes, however, is the weaving of seed bead jewelry.

This book is an introduction for newcomers to bead weaving, but it is also a conduit for experienced bead weavers who are looking for ways to make their woven jewelry unique. Too many times, the seed beading art form is segregated from other jewelry techniques, such as wirework and bead stringing. The results are still beautiful, but they're also limiting. Jewelry makers can dramatically expand the type of seed bead jewelry they make by combining traditional seed bead techniques with a variety of other jewelry methods. From established seed bead stitches to a few simple wirework and stringing steps, this book shows beginners through advanced bead weavers how to make seed bead jewelry with designer flair. The projects in this book incorporate seed beads from Japan and the Czech Republic with gemstones, pearls, crystals, and wire components. You'll also find an extensive technique section with step-by-step illustrations, jewelry projects combining all the stitches and methods described in the book, and a gallery displaying work from a host of talented jewelry artists.

Bead weaving is not a difficult or arcane pursuit; it is an exciting and accessible art form anyone can enjoy. You only need some magical beads and a needle and thread to get started.

CHAPTER ONE
BEADS AND SUPPLIES

About Seed Beads

Seed beads are available in a mind-boggling assortment of finishes, sizes, colors, and cuts. This is wonderful for bead lovers, but it can also be overwhelming, even for the most experienced of bead weavers, when trying to select beads for a specific jewelry project. It is a good idea to become familiar with at least some of the different types of seed beads on the market. Small differences, such as a matte finish or a hex cut, can affect the outcome of a jewelry design.

Seed Bead Sizes

Although it may seem like all seed beads are just plain tiny, they actually come in different sizes—ranging from the largest, at approximately 4 mm to the smallest, at approximately 1.5 mm. Each size seed bead has a number assigned to it rather than a diameter. For example, size 11 is approximately 2.2 mm in diameter and is the most popular size.

Here is a list of other popular seed bead sizes and their approximate diameters in millimeters:

Size 6	=	4 mm
Size 8	=	3 mm
Size 11	=	2.2 mm
Size 12	=	1.8 mm
Size 15	=	1.5 mm

Seed Bead Types

Most seed beads come from either the Czech Republic or Japan. There are pros and cons for each country's beads. Czech beads are not as uniform as Japanese seed beads, and sometimes their holes are small. However, they come in some colors that aren't always available in Japanese beads, and they are also more economical. Purchased by the hank, which means they are temporarily strung on nylon or silk cord with as many as ten or twelve strings of beads per hank, the number of size 11 beads per hank averages 4,000. The price range varies (depending on the finish) from $3 to $5 USD ($2.50 to $4 EUR).

Japanese seed beads are sold by the gram, usually in plastic tubes or small plastic bags. Vendors buy these by the kilo, and then divide them up, so the packaging can vary, as can the number of grams per package. Because of their uniform size, Japanese beads are higher quality than Czech beads, making them much easier to weave with, especially for beginners. Prices vary depending on the finish, the bead size, the manufacturer, and the gram weight. On average, a package of size 11 Japanese seed beads can cost anywhere from $2 to $6 USD ($1.50 to $5 EUR).

Seed Bead Colors

Cosmetic companies and seed bead manufacturers have one thing in common when it comes to colors: they each like to come up with unique names. Red seed beads may not simply be called "red." They may be "brick red" or "cherry." Names and colors vary tremendously depending on where the beads are made. No matter what they are called, you'll find a huge assortment of colors available.

Seed Bead Finishes

One of the elements that distinguishes one seed bead from another—other than size—is the finish. It is not unusual to have a combination of finishes on one bead, such as opaque matte, iris transparent, or translucent color-lined. Also, depending on the manufacturer, some terms can be used interchangeably. For example, aurora borealis (usually shortened to AB) is a term used to describe the same finish as that of iris and rainbow. Below is a list of some of the more popular seed bead finishes.

 COLOR-LINED ■ The bead is transparent but lined on the inside with a color. For example, a bead may be purple transparent on the outside but have a yellow lining on the inside.

 CYLON ■ This finish gives a pearly look to the bead, so it is a little shiny. Pastel and white seed beads often have a cylon finish on them.

GALVANIZED ■ These beads have a shiny appearance. The word *galvanized* refers to the process that coats the outside of the bead. Although they are beautiful, be careful. Manufacturers recommend that jewelry woven with these beads have a clear fixative (available from companies such as Krylon) sprayed on to keep the finish from rubbing off.

 IRIS ■ An iris finish creates a rainbow effect so that there are different shades of color and a little sparkle.

 LUSTER ■ Like the iris finish, luster adds a shiny, iridescent look to a bead.

 MATTE ■ These beads are frosted, so they aren't smooth like many seed beads. They are a good way to add some texture to a piece of jewelry, but their finish can cause some difficulty with weaving as they can be challenging to hold against each other while working.

 METALLIC ■ A metal finish, similar to that on galvanized beads, looks great, but usually needs to have a clear fixative applied to help resist wear.

 OPAQUE ■ These beads are a solid color that is not penetrable with light.

 RAINBOW ■ Similar to an iris finish, a rainbow finish creates a kaleidoscope of colors.

 SILVER-LINED ■ Silver-lined beads have a silver lining inside the bead.

 TRANSLUCENT ■ Some light is visible through these beads because they are clear and tinted with color.

Seed Bead Shapes

With most beads, round is the first shape that comes to mind. True, most seed beads are round, but they also come in a number of other shapes.

BUGLE ■ Tubular-shaped bugles come in different lengths, normally from 1/2 inch up to 2 inches (1.3 to 5 cm). Bugle beads work well with the ladder stitch and in fringe.

DELICA ■ These beads are shaped like short cylinders and are primarily used for the peyote stitch. The term *Delica* refers to a brand of these beads. Most weavers refer to these types of beads by the brand name Delica, even though similar brands include Aikos and Magnificas. They are manufactured in Japan and are approximately the same size as a size 11 seed bead, though sometimes they are referred to as size 12.

FRINGE ■ As the name suggests, these teardrop-shaped beads are good to use on the ends of fringe.

HEX CUT ■ Also referred to as two-cut, hex cut beads have six faceted sides.

ROUND ■ This is the most popular shaped seed bead, and it is available in a huge variety of colors and finishes.

SQUARE ■ Just as with the round beads, square-shaped seed beads come in many colors and finishes. Include them in fringe, in necklace straps, or in stitches such as free-form sculptural peyote and Dutch spiral.

TRIANGLE ■ Another way to add dimension to a design, triangle-shaped seed beads work well with the free-form sculptural peyote and Dutch spiral stitches or as accents in necklace straps and fringe.

TWISTED BUGLE ■ These are the same as regular bugles, but twisted bugle beads have a twisted, textured surface.

Related Supplies

Beads are not all that is needed to bead weave. There are a number of other supplies that are necessary. To get started, you'll need a few of the basics.

(A) BEAD TRAYS ■ While weaving, a bead tray is handy for holding all the beads used for a project. Look for shallow trays or bowls, preferably with multiple compartments. The shallow divided compartments make it easier to scoop lots of beads onto a needle at once. Most bead vendors have an assortment of trays available, but also check local discount stores for kitchen items such as chip and dip trays.

(B) BEESWAX OR THREAD HEAVEN ■ To condition Nymo thread, unravel the amount needed for a project, and rub it across either beeswax or a product called Thread Heaven. This will help keep threads from tangling.

(C) NEEDLE CASE ■ Needles come packaged in multiples, anywhere from ten to a few dozen per package. It's important to have a safe and secure place to keep all weaving needles. A small wooden needle case is great for storing needles when not in use.

(D) INTERFACING ■ For beaded embroidery, thick interfacing helps provide body to the piece. There are a few brands available, but for beading, a brand called Stiff Stuff is one of the most popular.

(E) SUEDE SCRAPS ■ After a piece is beaded with the beaded embroidery technique, most bead weavers like to finish the back by gluing and then sewing on a piece of suede, leather, or ultra-suede. Scrap pieces are available at most fabric stores and beading suppliers.

(A) NEEDLES ■ Bead weaving needles differ from sewing needles in that they are longer, usually a few inches (or millimeters) in length, and thinner. As with seed beads, needles have numbers that indicate their thickness. The smaller the number, the thicker the needle. For most bead weaving projects, sizes 10 to 13 work best. Try out a few different lengths and diameters to see which you prefer, but stick to quality needles. Beading needles from England are some of the highest quality needles available.

(B) BEAD SCOOPER ■ Not 100 percent necessary, but very handy, small metal scoopers work well when transferring tiny beads back and forth from a beading tray to a storage container.

(C) SCISSORS ■ Invest in a good pair of small, sharp scissors, and in order to keep them in good condition, don't use them for anything but bead work.

(D) THREADS ■ With so many types of threading medium available today, it would be easy to write an entire book about thread. The projects in this book use two of the most common bead weaving threads: either Nymo or Silamide. Nymo is nylon and is packaged on either small bobbin-sized spools or larger bulk spools. It is available in a wide assortment of colors and half a dozen thicknesses.

From thinnest to thickest, they include: OO, O, A, B, C, and D. Nymo is the favorite of many experienced bead weavers, but Silamide has started to catch up over the years. It is made of two-ply twisted nylon and comes pre-waxed, which is one reason it has become so popular. Nymo requires conditioning with beeswax or a product called Thread Heaven; otherwise, it can tangle easily. Silamide is packaged on either large 900-yard (823 m) sewing spools or 100-yard (92 m) cards, and usually comes in only one thickness (size A), and is available in a wide range of colors.

(E) VELVET PAD ■ Some bead weavers enjoy working on a velvet pad (like the kind used in stores to display fine jewelry). The nap on the pad keeps beads from rolling around too much.

BEAD STORAGE (NOT SHOWN) ■ New products for storing beads continually come on the market. Most seed beads are packaged in either bags or tubes, but then you need someplace to put them, as well as loose beads. Besides the commercial storage units available, plastic utility boxes (the kind used by fishermen) work well, as do stackable round jars or storage containers with lots of small clear drawers (used by mechanics to store nuts and screws). Browse through local hardware stores to find economical bead storage options.

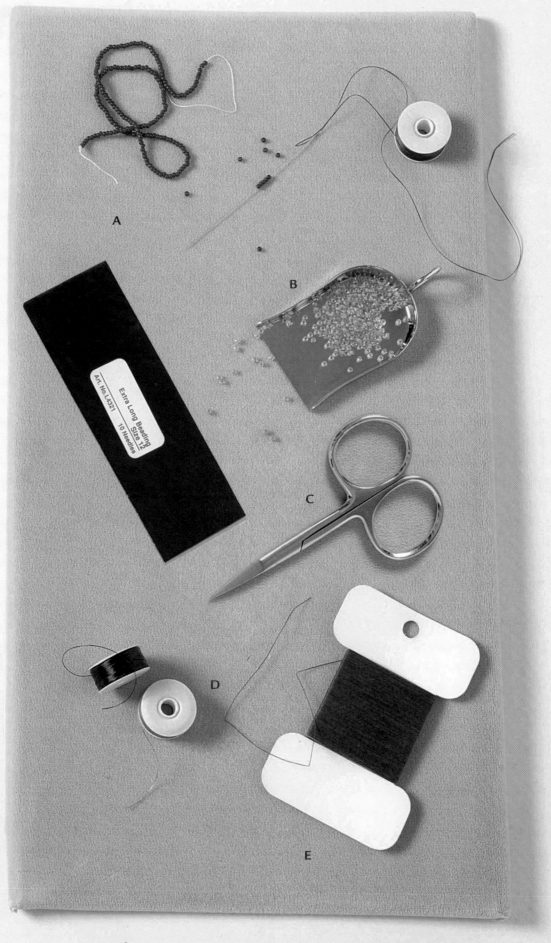

A

Art. No. L4321
Extra Long Beading
Size 12
10 Needles

B

C

D

E

15525330

CHAPTER TWO
SEED BEAD AND RELATED JEWELRY TECHNIQUES

This section provides step-by-step illustrated instructions for ten popular bead weaving stitches: ladder, Comanche (also known as brick), even count flat peyote, free-form sculptural peyote, bead embroidery, Dutch spiral, double needle weave, single thread netting, square stitch, and chevron. These stitches offer a variety of design options for the bead weaver, and are easy to execute with a little practice.

Bead weaving stitches are central to learning how to make seed bead jewelry, but in order to construct functional jewelry designs, it is also necessary to understand different procedures for starting and ending jewelry pieces. Just as with any type of jewelry making, seed bead jewelry requires some practical items like clasps and toggles. Embellishments, such as straps and fringe, are also important for making a piece of seed bead jewelry look finished. This section will explain the nuts and bolts of making a piece of jewelry you can wear with confidence. Finally, a wire components instruction section is provided, again combining function with fashion. Basic findings, including jump rings and ear hooks, are simple to make and add an artistic touch to your finished designs.

After you feel comfortable with a new stitch or two, move on to the Jewelry Projects section of this book. There, you'll discover how to combine traditional seed bead techniques with other jewelry methods and materials, such as gemstones and crystals, dramatically expanding the variety of seed bead jewelry you can create.

Beginnings and Endings

Along with mastering a few bead weaving stitches, there are a number of other techniques that are necessary for constructing actual jewelry pieces. These methods are used to start and finish jewelry items, and, while none of them are very difficult to learn, they are important to give a finished piece of jewelry a polished look. Nothing can be more unattractive in a woven piece of jewelry than loose threads or awkwardly attached clasps. These more minor techniques are also helpful in adding that little extra something to the overall design. With a handcrafted wire clasp, for example, you are able to combine a different medium with your seed beads. A beaded toggle provides a way to sneak in a gemstone here and there. This section includes methods for beginning and ending the jewelry projects in this book. However, this is just a smattering of construction techniques available to the bead weaver.

Conditioning Thread

Some beading threads, such as Nymo, need to be conditioned by coating the thread with beeswax or Thread Heaven. This helps keep the thread from tangling as you weave.

1. Start by using your thumb to hold a strand of Nymo against a piece of beeswax or Thread Heaven, and pull the strand with your other hand.

2. Coat the thread two or three times for best results.

Threading a Needle

Threading a beading needle can sometimes drive a new bead weaver a little crazy. Because these needles are thinner than regular sewing needles, it requires a different approach. You will need a pair of sharp scissors, your choice of threading medium, and a beading needle.

1. Cut the thread and **condition** it with beeswax or Thread Heaven if using Nymo rather than Silamide thread.

2. Hold the end of the thread between your thumb and index finger, exposing a very small amount of thread.

3. While holding the thread vertically, hold the needle in the other hand horizontally and bring the eye of the needle down over the end of the thread.

4. If you have trouble getting the eye over the thread, try turning the needle around to the other side and repeat step 3. (Needles have a right and a wrong side to them.)

Using a Stop Bead

A stop bead, also referred to as a tension bead, is used to stop beads from slipping off the thread when beginning a stitch. This is a simple, yet very handy technique. Along with a threaded beading needle, you just need one seed bead. It's helpful to use a stop bead that doesn't match the beads used in the stitch because you will remove this bead later, after completing a few rows.

1. After threading a needle, bring the needle up through a seed bead.

2. Take the needle down and back up through the bottom of the same bead, leaving a thread tail, usually a minimum of 6" (15.2 cm) in length.

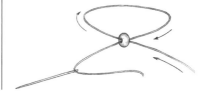

3. After finishing the stitch or a few rows and you feel the stitch is secure, just pull the stop bead off of the thread.

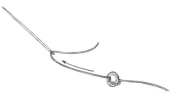

Adding Thread

While weaving most jewelry items, it becomes necessary to add more thread as the piece evolves. Keep a pair of sharp scissors and the selected thread medium handy while working on a project. Few jewelry pieces can be completed with one single strand of Nymo or Silamide.

1. Locate a bead that is close to where you need your working thread to exit, but also make sure you don't plan to go through this bead later. You don't want to fill up beads with too much thread. This can make it more difficult, or even impossible, to pass through the needle and thread again.

2. Once you've selected a bead to enter, insert the newly threaded needle into this bead, leaving a thread tail about 6" (15.2 cm) long

(unless a project specifies a longer tail). Begin to snake it up through other beads in the piece as you make your way to the bead you plan to exit.

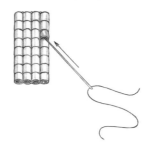

3. After snaking it through a few beads, you'll start to notice the threads that attach the previously woven beads together. These are sometimes referred to as bridge threads.

4. Select a bridge thread, insert your needle and thread around it, tie a simple overhand knot, and pull the

thread so that the knot slides into the nearest bead.

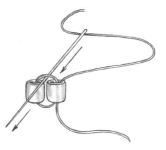

5. Continue to snake the needle toward your exit bead. If you have a large area of beads to snake through, you may want to knot the thread again. Otherwise, just keep snaking and finish by inserting the needle through the exit bead. At this point, you should be in position to continue the original stitch.

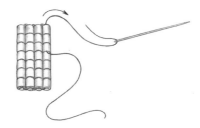

Finishing Thread

As you work a piece, you'll start to accumulate various pieces of extra thread. Also, at times, you will need to finish off the working thread in order to get a new, longer piece of thread. Remember, to complete a piece, most projects require that you leave a 6" (15 cm) thread tail when beginning a stitch or adding a new working thread to a piece. It's necessary at some point, (normally when you've completed a jewelry piece), to finish off these extra threads by tucking them back up into the beads. For this you will need a beading needle and pair of scissors.

1. If a thread tail is already knotted (see **adding thread**, previous page), attach a needle to the thread, and snake the needle and thread it through previously woven beads until you have all but about an inch or so of thread left. Then

use sharp scissors to trim off the excess thread.

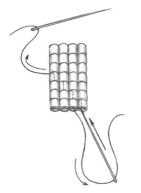

2. If you need to finish off a working thread, rather than a thread tail, locate a bead that is closest to where the thread is exiting, and insert the needle into this bead.

3. Continue to snake the needle and thread through a few beads. You'll start to notice the threads that are attaching the previously woven beads together. These are sometimes referred to as "bridge threads."

4. Select a bridge thread, insert your needle and thread around it, tie a simple over-

hand knot, and pull the thread so the knot slides into the nearest bead.

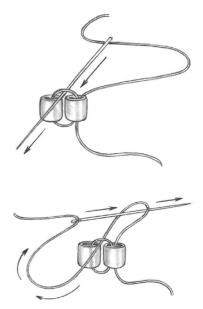

5. Continue to snake the needle through the beaded piece. If you have a large area of beads to snake through, you may want to knot again. Otherwise, just keep snaking and finish by exiting the needle through one of the beads previously woven. Then use sharp scissors to trim off excess thread.

Bead Tips

Findings called bead tips, also known as clamshells, provide a good way to start some jewelry projects, both with bead weaving and with regular bead stringing. These are metal findings, available in base metals as well as sterling silver, gold, and gold-filled. The hooks attached to the bead tips are used to attach a clasp after a jewelry piece is constructed. The tools needed for attaching bead tips include flat-nosed pliers, scissors, jeweler's glue, and a corsage pin or an awl. For seed-beaded jewelry, you also need two seed beads no larger than size 11, one for each bead tip.

1. After threading a needle, tie two overhand knots, one on top of the other. On the end, string on one seed bead, and push it down to the end of the thread.

2. Insert the needle back through the bottom of the seed bead (you'll notice this is similar to the **stop bead** technique), pushing the bead up against the knot.

3. Insert the needle down through the hole in the middle of the bead tip, and pull the cord so that the knots and seed bead rest inside one of the shells.

4. Trim off the excess cord, and drop a small amount of glue onto your knots.

5. Use flat-nosed pliers to close the two shells of the bead tip together.

6. When you are ready to finish off with the next bead tip, add another one to the end of your jewelry piece by slipping the needle and thread through the hole in the bead tip so that the open part of the bead tip (the shells) faces away from the beads previously strung.

7. String on another seed bead, bring the needle up through the bottom of the bead, and push the bead down into the cup of the bead tip.

8. Tie a loose, overhand knot with your thread, insert a corsage pin or a beader's awl into the knot, and push the knot down into the bead tip and up against the seed bead. Repeat this.

9. Trim off the excess thread, and drop a small amount of glue into the bead tip shell.

10. Finish by using flat-nosed pliers to close the two shells of the bead tip together.

Crimp Beads

Like the bead tip, a crimp bead is a finding used to finish off the ends of beaded jewelry. For the purposes of most seed bead jewelry, crimp beads are often used with beading wire. Some of the projects in this book use bead stringing techniques in combination with bead weaving stitches. This is when crimp beads become very useful. To use this method, you need a pair of crimping pliers, crimp beads, round-nosed pliers, wire cutters, and beading wire. Tube crimp beads are easier to work with than round ones.

1. Slide one crimp bead onto the end of a piece of beading wire, and loop the wire back through the crimp bead.

2. Position the crimp bead inside the second notch in the crimping pliers (the one closest to you when you are holding the pliers in your hand), and close the pliers around the bead. You should see that the crimp bead now has a groove down the middle so that it curls.

3. Now position the same crimp bead in the first notch in the pliers, and close the pliers around it so that you flatten the curl.

4. Use wire cutters to trim off all but about 1/4" (6 mm) of excess beading wire.

5. Add your beads, making sure you slide the first bead over both pieces of wire on the end.

6. Once you have all of your beads on, you are ready to finish the other end. Slide a second crimp bead onto the end of your wire so that it comes after the last strung bead.

7. Loop the wire back through the crimp bead as well as the last bead of the piece.

8. Insert the nose of your round-nosed pliers into the loop.

9. While holding your round-nosed pliers with one hand, gently pull the beading wire with your other hand so that you push the crimp bead up against the other beads. This will ensure that you do not have any extra slack in your beaded piece and that you also keep the end loop of your beading wire intact.

10. Repeat steps 2 and 3 above to close the crimp bead.

11. Finish by using the wire cutters to carefully trim off the excess beading wire.

Beaded Loop Straps

One strap method, which is very useful for amulets, is to make a loop of beads on the end. This way, the loops can either be stitched closed around other loops for a permanent strap (see the Petite Pearl Peyote Amulet project), or you can attach wire hooks to the loops to make a detachable strap. Necessary supplies for this technique include scissors, a wire wrapped hook or an amulet bead loop, jeweler's cement, beads, and a needle and thread.

1. With a few yards of thread on the beading needle, pull the thread through until it is doubled in thickness.

2. String on some seed beads—anywhere from 10 to 15 is a good amount, depending on the beads and the jewelry project—and push the beads down to about 6" (15.2 cm) from the end of the doubled thread.

3. Insert the beaded thread through a wire **wrapped hook** or an **amulet bead loop** before continuing.

4. Insert the needle through the first strung bead and continue inserting until you reach the last strung bead. Then pull the beads and threads to form a loop.

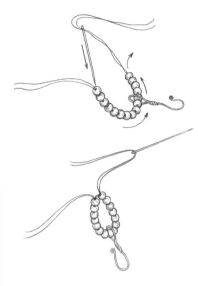

5. Continue to snake the needle and thread through the bead loop at least one more time to reinforce it.

6. With the tail and strap threads, tie a square knot.

7. Dab a little jeweler's cement onto the knot and allow it to dry before adding beads to the strap.

8. When you start to add beads to the strap, insert the thread tail up through a few of the beads and then trim off the excess thread with scissors.

9. Continue adding beads to the strap to create the desired length, and then repeat steps 1 through 8 to make another bead loop on the other end of the strap.

Amulet Beaded Loops

One way to attach a strap to an amulet is to add beaded loops on either side of the amulet. These loops then allow for a number of options. You can create a detachable strap, or you can attach a permanent strap to the loops. To make beaded loops, you need beads, a needle, and thread.

1. Begin by using the **adding thread** technique to attach a thread onto one side of the amulet.

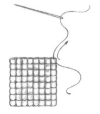

2. String on the desired number of beads. Anywhere from ten to fifteen beads is a good range, depending on the size of the beads.

3. Insert the needle back into the same bead from which the thread extends.

4. To reinforce the loop, snake the needle and thread back through the loop a few times before finishing the thread with the **finishing thread** technique.

Basic Fringe

Although there are enough variations on fringe to fill an entire book, most weavers start with this basic fringe technique. Fringe is useful as an embellishment on amulets, earrings, and necklaces. To make fringe, you'll need a needle and thread as well as a selection of seed beads, and other beads such as crystals.

1. Position the working thread so it is coming out of a bead in the spot where you want the strand of fringe to be placed.

2. Thread on your choice of beads (teardrops work really well for this), and make sure you end with one seed bead.

3. Skipping the last seed bead, insert the needle back through the beads previously strung and into the same bead from which the thread extends.

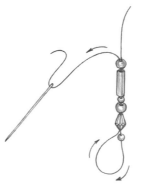

4. After adding all the desired fringe, finish with the **finishing thread** technique.

Stitch Tip

*Varying the types of fringe you use can give a jewelry design a completely new look. Basic fringe and swag fringe are covered in this book, but there are lots of other fringe variations, such as **branch fringe** and **twisted fringe**. Once you acquire a few fringe techniques continue to learn more fringe variations so you can easily alter woven jewelry designs just by using a different method.*

Beaded Toggles

Metal toggle clasps are popular jewelry findings, but you can also use beads to create your own toggles. You just need to select one large bead, usually about 6 to 10 mm depending on the jewelry piece, and then make a loop of seed beads to fasten around the bead. In addition to the large bead, you will need a needle and thread and seed beads.

1. For the large bead side of the toggle, make sure the working thread is anchored in the spot where you want the toggle to be located, and then string on a few seed beads. The number of beads is up to you, but five is usually a good choice.

2. String on the large bead and one more seed bead.

3. Take the needle, and skipping the last seed bead, insert it back through the large bead and the seed beads added in step 1.

4. Reinforce this by snaking the needle and thread back through the beads just strung, again inserting it back down and skipping the last seed bead.

5. Use the **finishing thread** technique to remove the working thread.

6. For the other side, make sure the working thread is in the right location (using the

adding thread technique, if necessary), and string on enough seed beads to create a loop that will fit around the large bead previously attached.

7. Insert the needle back into the same bead from which the thread extends, constructing a loop.

8. Reinforce the loop by snaking the needle and threading it back through the loop a few times before finishing the thread with the **finishing thread** technique.

Swag Fringe

Also referred to as looped fringe, swag fringe is a variation of basic fringe. Instead of bringing the needle back up through the beads to create a straight piece of fringe, you bring it up through another bead to form a loop, or swag effect. Just as with basic fringe, this technique requires thread, a needle, and your choice of beads.

1. Position the working thread so it is coming out of a bead in the spot where you want the strand of fringe to be placed.

2. Thread on your choice of beads, and insert the needle through the bottom of one of the beads in the same row.

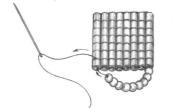

3. After adding all the desired fringe, finish with the **finishing thread** technique.

Whipstitch

This is a common sewing stitch. It is used in bead weaving to sew beaded pieces together and to attach items such as suede to the back of beaded jewelry components, which are often glued onto interfacing. If you've ever done any hand sewing, then you are probably already familiar with this stitch.

1. Tie a knot on the end of the thread, and bring the needle up through the two items you are stitching together. For example, this might be interfacing and suede.

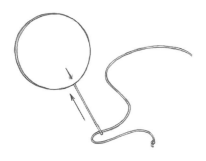

2. Bring the needle around to the back of the pieces, where you originally threaded the needle, and again, insert the needle and thread through the two pieces.

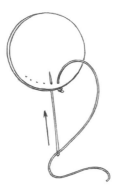

3. Continue this until you work all around the items you're stitching together, and then finish off the thread by tying

an overhand knot in one of the last stitches made.

4. Snake the needle between the two pieces stitched together, and trim off the excess thread.

Wire Components

Wire is one of the most versatile jewelry mediums available. Even if you don't have much experience working with metal, many wire techniques just take a little practice, and you'll soon be able to add a unique twist to your bead weaving designs. Learn to make ear hooks, jump rings, or even clasps to finish off a handcrafted piece of jewelry. Some of the basic tools needed for these techniques include round-nosed pliers, flush-cut wire cutters, jeweler's files, nylon-nosed pliers, and flat- or bent-nosed pliers. Although you should feel free to experiment with different types of wire, half-hard round (sterling silver or gold-filled) wire in gauges ranging from 22 to 20 is a good place to start for the findings listed below. The hardness of the wire will help keep its shape, which is especially important for clasps, but it is still fairly easy to manipulate with your fingers and a few hand tools. Wire measurements are provided for each wire finding below as a guide to illustrate the average amount of wire needed for each component. I find it much easier to work with more rather than less wire. About 6" (15.2 cm) is a good length to work with. It's always better to have a little extra than not enough. For more wire finding projects, take a look at my book *Making Designer Bead and Wire Jewelry* (Quarry Books, 2005). If you don't feel ready to dig into a little wirework right away, don't worry. There are tons of wonderful prefabricated findings available from bead vendors, both online and in bead shops.

S-Hook Clasp

The S-hook clasp is about the easiest clasp to make, and you only need about 2" (5.1 cm) of 20-gauge wire, a jeweler's file, and round-nosed pliers. Use these clasps to connect **amulet beaded loops** together, or connect each end to **jump rings** for a quick clasp solution.

1. Start by using a jeweler's file to smooth the ends of the wire.

2. Place the nose of the round-nosed pliers a little higher than halfway down the wire, and curl one end of the wire around the nose to create a hook shape.

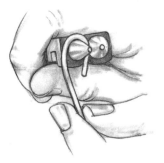

3. Repeat step 2 on the other end of the wire so that the hook is facing the opposite direction.

4. Use the round-nosed pliers to make the smallest possible curls on both ends of the wire.

Jump Rings

Jump rings are one of the most adaptable of all jewelry findings. You can purchase precut jump rings from many suppliers, but it's not that difficult to make your own. You just need a wooden dowel (or a pencil), flush-cut wire cutters, a jeweler's file, and about 6" (15.2 cm) of 20-gauge wire.

1. Begin by using your fingers to wrap the wire around the dowel (or pencil) so that the wire is flush against it.

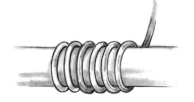

2. Slide the wire off the dowel so that you have a coil of wire.

3. With a pair of flush-cut wire cutters, cut each coil once to create a single ring.

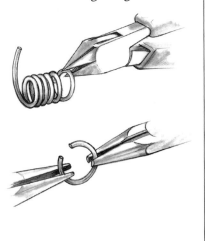

4. Finally, use a jeweler's file to smooth the ends of the wire so that both ends of the jump ring are flat and can fit flush together.

Basic Ear Hooks

Make your own earring hooks with either 21- or 22-gauge half-hard round wire. While some wire workers prefer 20 gauge for ear wires, this is sometimes too thick to get through an ear hole. Along with a few basic hand tools, you need a 3 1/2" (8.9 cm) length of wire.

1. Begin by cutting your wire in half so that you have two pieces that are 1³/₄" (4.5 cm) each. Then use a jeweler's file to file the ends of each piece.

2. With round-nosed pliers, create a small loop on one end of one piece of wire.

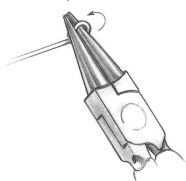

3. Repeat step 2 for your other piece of wire, ensuring that the second loop is the same size as the first.

4. Next, hold both pieces of wire together so that the loops are lined up right next to each other.

5. With the thickest part of your round-nosed pliers, grasp the straight part of your wires approximately ¹/₄" (6 mm) past the loops, and use your fingers to bend both wires 180 degrees around the nose. You want to bend both wires at the same time to make your ear wires match.

continued

6. The next step is a very small, subtle movement, but it will help you make the hook a little more rounded. Using your round-nosed-pliers, position the largest part of the nose inside the bent area, approximately ¼" (6 mm) from the curl. The pliers' nose should point up and the wire curl should be positioned horizontally toward you. Gently push the curl away from you so that you are bending the wire about 5 degrees.

7. Hold both ear hooks side by side again. This time, use the middle area on the nose of your pliers and, measuring about ¼" (6 mm) away from

the ends, slightly bend the ends of both wires (approximately 25 degrees) at the same time.

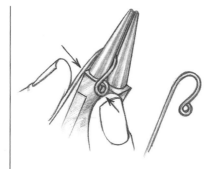

Beaded Ear Hooks

Once you learn to make *basic ear hooks*, you can try this variation. The steps are almost identical, but this way you get to sneak an extra couple of beads into your design. What could be better? You'll need almost the same supplies, plus a few beads to add to the ear hook, and 4" (10.2 cm) of 21- or 22-gauge wire. Before starting these ear hooks, double-check that the wire fits through the selected beads.

1. Begin by cutting your wire in half so that you have two pieces that are 2" (5.1 cm) each. Then use a jeweler's file to file the ends of each piece.

2. As described in steps 2 and 3 of the **basic ear hooks**, make a small loop on each piece of wire.

3. Now slip one bead onto each piece of wire, and push the bead up against the loops you just made.

4. As described in step 5 of the **basic ear hooks** (above), take one of the wire and bead pieces and wrap the wire around your round-nosed pliers, but this time, position the pliers ¼" (6 mm) from the bead that is resting next to your loop.

5. Repeat the previous step for your second ear hook.

6. Again, referring to the instructions above for the **basic ear hooks**, follow steps 6 and 7 for each ear hook to make complete pair.

Wrapped Hook

Very similar to the **S-hook clasp**, this variation has an S on one end and a wrapped loop on the other end. When using this type of clasp, it's important to consider whether you'll need to attach an element, such as a bead loop of some kind, to the wrapped area. Depending on the design, sometimes it's necessary to start the wrap and then attach the item before finishing the wrap. You'll need almost the same supplies as for an S-hook clasp, plus 3" (7.6 cm) of 20-gauge wire and flat-nosed pliers.

1. Use a jeweler's file to smooth the ends of the wire.

2. As described in steps 2 and 4 of the **S-hook clasp** (previous page), use round-nosed pliers to create a hook and then a curl on one end of the wire.

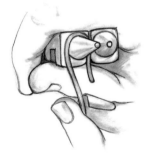

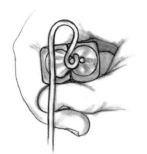

3. Use flat-nosed pliers to bend the wire 90 degrees, creating an upside-down L shape.

4. Position the round-nosed pliers in the bend created in the previous step, and use your fingers or flat-nosed pliers to grasp the wire and wrap it around to form a loop.

5. Continue to hold the loop with round-nosed pliers, and, with one finger, press the loop against the nose. As you hold this in one hand, use the other hand to wrap the loose wire around the straight piece of wire that is directly under the loop. Use your fingers or flat-nosed pliers, depending on the softness of the wire.

6. Once you've wrapped the wire a few times, trim off any excess wire, and use the flat-nosed pliers to press the wire-wrapped end flat to ensure it doesn't scratch the wearer.

7. If necessary, use round-nosed pliers to straighten the loop.

Figure-Eight Eye

It hardly takes any wire to make this component, which is shaped like a figure eight and used to connect strands to all types of hook-style clasps. You need about 1½" (3.8 cm) of 20-gauge wire, but of course, you can make this bigger or smaller with different lengths of wire. You'll also need a jeweler's file and round-nosed pliers.

1. Start by using a jeweler's file to smooth both ends of the wire.

2. Now, use your round-nosed pliers to make a large loop on one end of the wire so that you have used up half of the piece of wire.

3. Do the same on the other end of the wire, but, this time, the loop should be facing in the other direction so that you make a figure eight (8) with the wire.

Quadruple Loop Eye

This eye component resembles the petals of a flower. You can use it as you would the figure-eight eye to connect to hook-style clasps, or use your imagination to think of other ways to incorporate it into your seed bead designs. It requires about 4" (10.2 cm) of 20-gauge wire, round-nosed pliers, a jeweler's file, and wire cutters. It's also helpful to have a pair of nylon-nosed pliers handy to press the wire petals when finished.

1. Using round-nosed pliers, make a small loop on the end of a piece of wire.

2. Hold the wire with the round-nosed pliers and position the end of the nose against the first loop.

3. Make a second loop with your fingers by holding the straight part of the wire and wrapping it 180 degrees around the nose of the pliers.

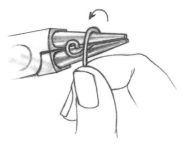

4. Repeat step 3 to make another loop.

5. Place the pliers' nose next to your third loop, and make a fourth loop right next to it.

6. Trim off the excess wire and file the end smooth.

7. Flatten the piece by gently compressing the finished eye with your nylon-nosed pliers.

Triple Loop Hook

This is a combination of the *quadruple loop eye* and the *S-hook clasp*. Team it up with a quadruple loop eye, or a *figure-eight eye,* or even a simple *jump ring*. You need about 3" (7.6 cm) of 20-gauge wire and round-nosed pliers.

1. Repeat steps 1 through 4 of the **quadruple loop eye.**

2. Repeat steps 1 and 2 from the **S-hook clasp** instructions, and use round-nosed pliers to make the smallest possible curl on the end of this hook.

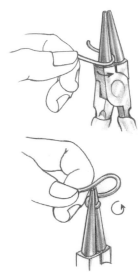

Bead Weaving Stitches

In many ways, bead weaving is comparable to needle arts, such as embroidery and needlepoint because, to create different types of designs, a bead weaver uses a variety of stitching techniques to connect the beads together. There are dozens of seed bead stitches, which is one reason why so many jewelry designers enjoy this art form. There's always something new to learn, and a huge assortment of methods to master. However, you don't need to become proficient at every stitch to get started. Once you learn even just one stitch, you can begin to create a variety of jewelry designs.

Ladder

MATERIALS

> your choice of seed beads or bugle beads (pictured in the illustrations below).

> needle and thread

Like the rungs of a ladder, this stitch, known as the ladder stitch, is very practical. It is one of the most useful stitches in bead weaving because it is often combined with other stitches such as *chevron* and *Comanche* (also known as brick stitch). Seed beads as well as bugle beads work well with this simple stitch technique. If you decide to use bugle beads, make sure you double-check that the ends of your beads are smooth as you weave on each bead. This can sometimes be a problem with low-quality bugle beads. The results are uneven or jagged edges, which can cut the thread.

1. Pick up two beads with the needle, and push them down the thread so that you leave approximately a 6" (15.2 cm) tail of thread (which you will weave in and finish off later to complete a design).

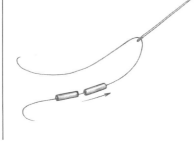

2. Insert the needle back up through the bottom of the first bead.

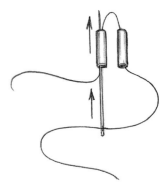

continued

3. Then insert the needle back down through the second bead, and gently pull on the thread so that both beads align themselves side by side.

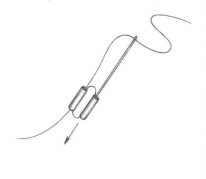

4. Add a third bead, then insert the needle down through the second bead and back up through the bottom of the third bead.

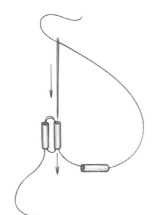

5. At this point, you now have three "rungs" of your ladder stitched together. Repeat step 4 until you have the desired length, which depends on the jewelry design you're constructing.

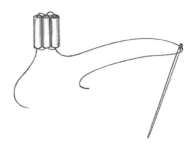

Comanche (also known as Brick)

MATERIALS

> ladder-stitched bead piece

> your choice of seed beads

> needle and thread

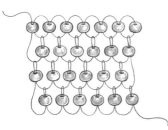

As the name indicates, Comanche stitch is attributed to Native Americans. It is also commonly referred to as brick stitch and is used in combination with the *ladder stitch*. Before beginning the Comanche stitch, you'll first need

to make a ladder of beads the length you desire (see ladder stitch instructions). One interesting characteristic of this stitch is that it automatically forms a triangle shape as you work the stitch. Although it is possible to add and decrease beads to form different shapes other than triangles, you can do a great deal with the basics of this stitch.

1. Position the working thread so that it comes out of the first bead rung of the ladder piece. Normally, there will be enough thread to start the Comanche stitch right after doing the **ladder stitch**. Otherwise, bring the needle and thread up through the first rung of the ladder, making sure you leave a 6" (15.2 cm) tail of thread (which you

will weave in and finish off later to complete a design).

2. Notice that there is a piece of thread connecting each ladder rung. Add one seed bead to the needle, and then insert the needle through the thread that joins the first rung to the second rung.

3. Now bring the needle up through the bead you added in the previous step.

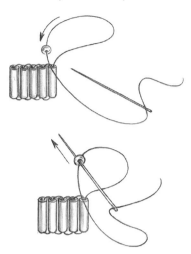

4. Pull the needle up as you use your fingers to push the bead down against the top of the ladder.

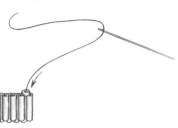

5. Repeat steps 2 through 4 until you have completed the first row of beads down the length of the ladder.

6. Turn the beaded piece around and continue to work from left to right, again repeating steps 2 through 4, but, this time, insert the needle through the thread between the seed beads in the first row rather than those on the ladder.

7. Continue this process until you have the desired width of beads you need for your jewelry project.

Even-Count Flat Peyote

MATERIALS
- Delica seed beads
- needle and thread

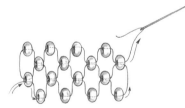

The peyote stitch (sometimes referred to as gourd stitch) is an extremely popular bead weaving stitch. While these instructions explain how to construct even count flat peyote, there are a number of peyote stitch variations, including odd count, round, and tubular. All are based on the basic idea of stringing on a bead, skipping a bead, and then passing the needle through the next bead in the row. Delica seed beads work wonderfully with this stitch because they are precisely cut, allowing the beads to fit tightly up against each other.

1. After threading the needle, add a **stop bead**.

2. String on the required number of beads, depending on the project, and pull them up against the **stop bead**. The number of beads will be an even number (thus the name "even count") and will be twice as many as you need for the first row. The reason for this will be clear after completing the next two steps.

3. Now string on one bead and, skipping one bead in the row previously strung, insert the needle through the next bead.

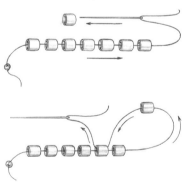

continued

4. Continue to string on a bead and skip a bead until the end of the row. As you work, you'll notice the beads are forming a pattern like the teeth in a zipper, or an up-and-down (one bead up and one bead down) pattern. At this point, you'll have three rows of peyote stitch completed because your first row turned into two rows as you added and skipped beads.

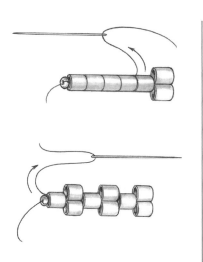

5. Flip the beaded piece around so you can continue to weave from right to left, following steps 3 and 4 above to add more peyote bead rows.

Free-Form Sculptural Peyote

MATERIALS

▸ your choice of beads

▸ needle and thread

It's hard to believe at first that free-form sculptural peyote and **even count flat peyote** are basically the same stitches. **Flat peyote** is so precise, resembling tiny little bricks neatly aligned next to each other, while free-form sculptural peyote seems to have no rhyme or reason to it. However, both of these stitches follow the same weaving concept: string a bead and skip a bead. The main difference between these stitches is in how you approach them. With free-form sculptural peyote, you can make up the rules as you weave. The idea is that as you weave you are sculpting a piece of jewelry that may twist and turn or lie on top of itself. Since there are no rules to this stitch, these instructions are only one way to approach free-form sculptural

peyote. Different bead weavers will have different methods. Try this one and see how it works for you, but then feel free to experiment and create your own method as well.

1. Start by selecting a color palette for your beads. You can find ideas for color combinations by flipping through an art book or browsing in a fabric store.

2. Once you have a range of colors determined, select two to four different types and colors of seed beads. These will help create the base of the sculptural piece.

3. Look through your bead stash for crystals, stones, metal pieces, and other beads that will also fit in with the color palette. Try to select a range of shapes and sizes.

4. Now you're ready to start the piece. Begin by making two to four rows of **even count flat peyote** using seed beads. Feel

free to mix up the seed bead colors. Remember that you aren't trying to create a symmetrical piece of jewelry.

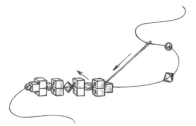

5. After you have a few seed bead rows started, you can start adding your other beads, such as crystals and stone beads, interspersing them with seed beads. Don't expect the beads to fit together the way they do in **flat peyote**. This is when the piece will start to take on unusual shapes.

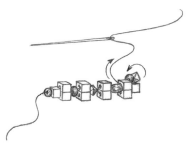

6. When you have some larger beads woven into the piece, the next technique to try is what I refer to as making a **bead bridge**. This will help integrate the larger beads into the design. String a number of seed beads onto the thread so that there are enough beads to fit around (to bridge

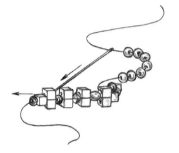

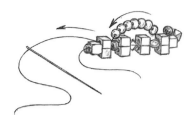

over) a larger bead in the previous row so that you can insert the needle into a seed bead that is positioned past this larger bead.

7. Another technique to try is to make small dangles of beads using the **basic fringe** method (described in the Beginnings and Endings section of this book).

8. Continue this process of interspersing different kinds of beads, making bridges here and there, and using the **even count flat peyote** stitch technique. You'll see your beaded sculpture grow and change as you work.

Beaded Embroidery

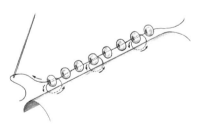

MATERIALS

- cabochon glued to interfacing
- your choice of beads
- needle and thread

The basic concept of beaded embroidery is very similar to that of regular embroidery, but you attach seed beads (to either cloth or interfacing, for example) as you stitch. This technique allows for infinite possibilities, from

beading dolls to creating wall hangings to embellishing jewelry pieces. These instructions explain one of the more popular methods of beaded embroidery used for jewelry: beading around a cabochon, which may be made of stone, glass, or porcelain. Specifically, the *couching* method, also referred to as a backstitch or running stitch, and the *picot edging* stitch are explained. Couching is used to bead around the cabochon, and the picot edging is a lacy effect used to cover the sides of a bead-embroidered cabochon.

1. For couching: Tie a knot on the end of the thread and insert the needle up through the back of the interfacing so the thread is positioned right next to the cabochon.

2. String on three or four seed beads, push them down against the interfacing, and use your thumb to push the beads up against the cabochon.

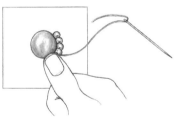

3. Insert the needle down through the interfacing immediately past the last seed bead.

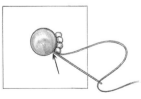

continued

4. Bring the needle back up through the back of the interfacing and in between two beads.

5. Insert the needle through the rest of the beads added in step 2.

6. Repeat steps 2 though 5 until you have a completed row of beads around the cabochon.

7. To help straighten the beads around the cabochon, snake the needle and thread back through all of the beads previously stitched.

8. To finish off the thread (if you don't want to make a picot edging), insert the needle through the back of the interfacing and tie a knot around one or two of the threads there. Then trim off the excess thread.

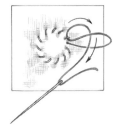

9. For picot edging: After going around the cabochon to help straighten the beads (as describe in step 7 above), the needle will be positioned so it is exiting one of the beads. String on three seed beads (five beads can also be used to create a larger ruffle effect, if desired).

10. Skip the next seed bead around the cabochon, and insert the needle through the next bead.

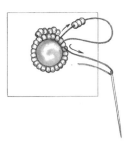

11. Continue to string on three seed beads and skip a bead until you have gone around the entire cabochon. Then follow step 8 to finish off the working thread.

Dutch Spiral

MATERIALS

> your choice of beads

> needle and thread

Peyote spiral and Dutch spiral are two terms for this stitch, which is really a variation of **peyote stitch**. After stringing on the first group of beads, the weaver ties the tail and working threads together to form a circle of beads; from then on, a tube of beads miraculously takes shape. It doesn't seem possible; even once you start this stitch, you'll have doubts. But after completing an inch (2.5 cm) or more, you'll see the results from your persistence and faith. These instructions explain how to use five types of beads to create the spiral, but you can use any number of bead types. The diameter of the finished spiral depends on the size of the beads and the number of different types of beads used in the stitch.

Some beaders like to double their thread for this stitch. This is up to you. A lot of beads make up a twist like this, so doubled thread is helpful for keeping the twist strong and the tension tight. Tension is critical for this stitch. If you do double the thread, make sure there's plenty of room for a double thickness of thread to pass through the bead holes. Always check this before deciding on which type of beads you plan to use.

1. Begin by deciding how many different types and sizes of beads you want to use. Usually, four or five different types work well. One type, however, should be seed beads; size 11 is a good choice. Beads will be strung in graduated sizes as you work around to create the spiral.

Therefore, the seed beads will always be the last beads strung.

2. Once you decide how many different sizes of beads to use, be prepared to buy a lot of beads. This stitch requires a lot of beads, but you'll find it well worth it when you see the results. You will especially need a large amount of the smallest beads (normally, size 11 seed beads).

3. Line up your beads from the largest to the smallest and assign each type a letter. For example, if you have five beads, the largest would be "A," the next smallest would be "B," and so on until the smallest. If you use five types of beads, seed beads are the smallest, and therefore would be "E."

A   B   C   D   E

4. Cut your choice of thread (Nymo or Silamide) and thread your needle.

5. Starting with the largest bead, string on one bead of each: A, B, C, and D.

6. Then string on five E beads (these are your size 11 seed beads).

7. String on another A bead (this is your largest bead).

8. Now tie these beads into a circle using a square knot, and leave a long tail, which you'll need to thread back into your finished piece later. (Long tails are also helpful if you want to attach a clasp or make a **beaded toggle** later on. So think about this when you start the tube.)

9. String on another A bead.

10. String on one B bead, and then go through the B bead in the previous row.

11. String on one C bead, and then go through the C bead in the previous row.

12. String on one D bead, and then go through the D bead in the previous row.

13. String on seven E beads (seed beads), and then go through the first seed bead in the previous row (not through all the seed beads). As you work this step, it is helpful to count the seed beads from the closest to the furthest, which is considered the first seed bead. Remember to keep the thread tension tight.

14. String on one A bead, then go through the A bead in the previous row.

continued

15. Repeat steps 10 through 14 with one change: when you get to the seed beads (the E beads), add two more for each row until you total eleven seed beads. From then on, you will use eleven of these beads in every row.

16. At this point, your piece may look really strange to you. However, have faith. As you work, pull your thread to tighten your beads. You'll see a little nest forming. Keep pulling the beads tightly as you work.

17. When you have reached the length you want, you are ready to decrease the seed beads (the E beads) for the last three rows. Therefore, use nine E beads for one row, then seven E beads for the next row, and then five E beads for the final row.

Double Needle Weave

MATERIALS

- your choice of beads
- two needles and thread
- two bead tips

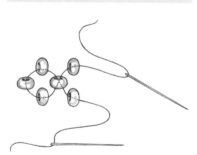

Two threaded needles are required for this stitch, so it can be a little tricky in the beginning not to get the threads tangled up. However, once you get going, you'll find this weaving stitch will work up fairly quickly. It's also important to make sure there's plenty of room for a double thickness of thread to pass through the bead holes. Always check this before deciding on which type of beads you plan to use. Along with seed beads, other beads to consider are pearls, crystals, and gemstone beads. Before weaving, you'll need to secure the thread ends. There are a few different ways to approach this, but a *bead tip* is one of the easiest ways to start and finish a *double needle weave* jewelry design.

1. Cut two pieces of thread approximately the same length, and thread both needles.

2. Attach a **bead tip** to the ends of both threads.

3. String one bead onto the right thread and two beads onto the left thread.

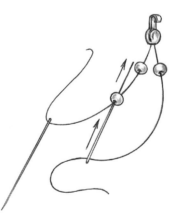

4. Insert the right needle (attached to the thread with one bead on it) up through the bottom of the second bead on the left thread.

5. Push all the beads up against the **bead tip**.

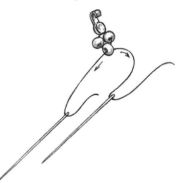

6. Repeat steps 3 through 5 until you have the desired length.

7. Then add one bead onto the left thread and one bead onto the right before finishing both ends with a **bead tip**.

Single Thread Netting

MATERIALS

> your choice of beads

> needle and thread

> bead tips

The netting stitch resembles old-fashioned nets used for catching fish. While those nets consisted of rope and a series of knots, the general idea with thread netting is just about the same, but instead of weaving with rope, you weave with beading thread and seed beads. Although there are a number of variations on this stitch, they developed from this basic method, which requires a single thread of beads, or a base row, to work from. Once the base row is established, you weave down the row, stringing on more beads and anchoring the working thread to the base row. The result is a web design, or netting, of beads. Because you don't have to create a solid piece of beadwork, you'll find this stitch works up really quickly. These instructions cover two approaches to netting stitch used for the projects in this book: one includes a small dangle at the end, and one includes just the beads, which form a loop or bead swag with no dangle in the middle.

1. Start by making the base row. There can be any number of beads in this row, depending on how long you want the piece to be, although it's best to determine ahead of time which beads will be used as the anchor areas on the row. When first learning this stitch, it's a good idea to make these anchor beads larger, or at least a different color, than the other beads on the base row. The **bead tip** technique works well for finishing both ends of the base row.

2. Once you have a base row ready to work with, you need an additional thread to make the netting. You can either use the adding threads technique to attach the additional thread to the base row, or you can include an additional thread with the base row before finishing the ends of the threads with a **bead tip**. Either method works. Just make sure you have the netting thread positioned in the area where you want to start the netting.

3. For netting with a dangle: On the netting thread, string on an odd number of beads, making sure you end with a seed bead. Crystals and teardrop-shaped beads are a nice touch here, so if you decide to use them, string one of these on as the second to last bead right before the final seed bead.

4. Skipping the last seed bead just strung, insert the needle up through a few of the other beads (not all of the beads, just a few). For example, if the last two beads before the final seed bead are a crystal and a pearl, insert the needle through these.

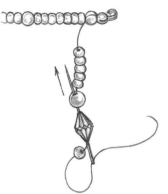

5. Except for the last two beads previously strung, string on the same number and types of beads strung on the first side of the dangle loop, and insert the needle through an anchor bead in the base row.

continued

6. Pull the thread to form the first netting loop. Continue stringing on beads, skipping the last seed bead, and anchoring to a bead in the base row, to complete the first netted row the full length of the base row.

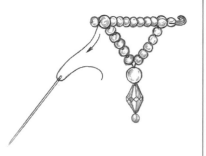

7. For netting without a dangle: On the netting thread, string on your choice of beads, and insert the needle through an anchor bead on the base row.

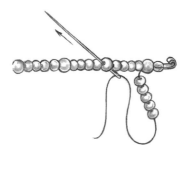

Square Stitch

MATERIALS

▸ Needle and thread

▸ Delica seed beads

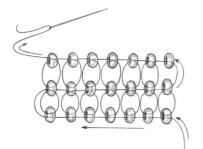

Square stitch can be used with any kind of seed beads, but Delica beads work best when first learning this stitch since the sides of the Delicas are more flat than round. This allows the beads to fit closely together. This stitch requires multiple needle and thread passes to help keep the beads aligned throughout the stitch. The following instructions first show how to make a two-bead wide square stitch pattern, which is a nice design for delicate items such as bracelets or amulet straps. Then the instructions progress to a four-bead wide square stitch pattern. You can continue to make this pattern as wide as you like by increasing the thickness with an even number of beads.

1. *Two-Bead Wide:* Add one Delica as if it was a **stop bead**, although it will be part of the stitch rather than pulled off at the end like most stop beads.

2. String on two more beads, and push them down against this first bead.

3. Bring the needle up and through the bottom of the second bead, and pull the thread so that the second bead rests up next to the third bead.

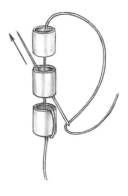

4. Bring the needle down through the top of the third bead.

5. String on a fourth bead, and bring the needle up through the first bead and then back down the top and through the fourth bead. All four beads will be locked together to form a small square.

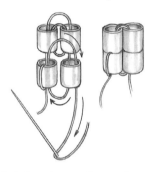

6. Bring the needle up through the first and second beads and then down through the third and fourth beads.

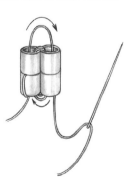

7. To continue the two-bead wide pattern, turn over the beaded piece so that the working thread is coming out of the last bead. To make a four-bead wide pattern, skip to step 10.

8. Then add one bead, and bring the needle up through the bead to the left of this bead and back down through the bead just added.

9. Continue to add a bead, and bring the needle through the bead to the left, flipping the beaded piece back and forth as you add beads to increase the length of the beaded piece.

10. *Four-Bead Wide:* String two beads onto the thread, and bring the needle through the bottom of the first bead and down through the top of the second bead.

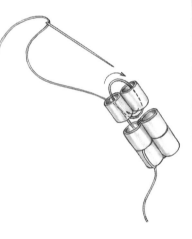

11. Keep bringing the needle down through the bead under the second bead, and then up through the bead to the left of the second bead.

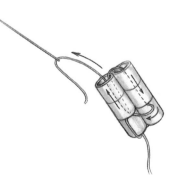

12. Repeat step 10. At this point, you've now created a four-bead wide square stitch pattern.

13. To lengthen the beaded piece, add one bead, and bring the needle up through the bead to the left and then back down through the bead just added.

14. After each row, bring the needle up and through the last two rows.

15. Flip the beaded piece so the working thread comes out from the top, and continue steps 13 and 14 until you have the desired length.

Chevron

MATERIALS

- › two ladder-stitched bead pieces
- › your choice of beads
- › needle and thread

The chevron stitch derives its name from the shape of a chevron, which is typically V shaped. It is not unusual to find different approaches to this stitch. There are, in fact, a number of bead weaving variations associated with the chevron stitch; however, they all have the shape of a V as part of the final woven pattern. The instructions provided below offer a single chevron pattern as well as an optional double chevron pattern. Unlike *peyote* or *square stitch*, chevron is much more forgiving when it comes to the type of beads it will tolerate. Czech beads are excellent to use with this stitch because their lack of uniformity will help create a three-dimensional, textured effect in the final woven piece.

1. For a single chevron pattern: This chevron stitch variation requires that you first create two equally long **ladder-stitched** pieces. You can use either bugle beads or seed beads for these.

2. Once you have two ladder-stitched pieces, use the **adding thread** technique and bring the needle up through one ladder rung on the end of one ladder section previously stitched.

3. Notice that there is a piece of thread connecting each ladder rung. You will be working your needle and thread through these sections (back and forth on both ladder pieces) to connect the two ladders together.

4. String on five seed beads, and then insert the needle through the thread that joins the first rung to the second rung on the second ladder piece.

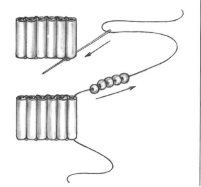

5. At this point, you should have one piece of thread with five seed beads connecting the two ladder pieces so that they mirror each other. Now insert the needle through the last strung seed bead. This will be the one closest to the second attached ladder piece and will work as the anchor bead.

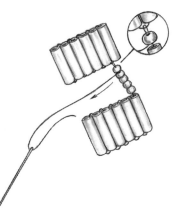

6. Pull the thread so all the beads are snug up against each other.

7. Now thread on four seed beads, skip a rung, and insert the needle through the next thread connection on the first ladder piece. This will be the first visual V pattern of beads.

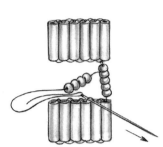

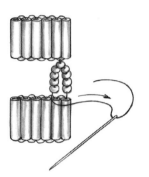

8. Again, just as in step 5 above, insert the needle through the last strung seed bead, and string on four more seed beads.

9. Continue this back and forth, inserting the needle through the last bead to form a V of beads, and skipping a rung to connect the two ladders together. When you finish, you will have one single layer of chevron stitch, and you can stop at this point.

10. For a double chevron pattern: If you want to add more texture to a piece, continue the same steps as above, but this time, move back down the two connected ladder pieces in the opposite direction, and only go through the thread rungs that you skipped while making the first chevron of beads.

11. Go through all the ladder thread rungs so that all the skipped ones have been attached. This will complete a double layer of chevron stitch.

CHAPTER THREE

JEWELRY PROJECTS

Admittedly, making jewelry with seed beads can be very time-consuming. However, a lot of time does not necessarily mean a lot of difficulty. I designed each project in this book around stitches that require a repetitive series of steps. Therefore, once you learn the stitch, you just need to repeat it over and over again to complete a piece of jewelry. Add in beautiful gemstone beads and sparkling crystals, and you will have a dazzling piece of jewelry that is deceptively simple to create. For a little more depth to your designs, you can fabricate some of your own findings with wire. The Beginnings and Endings section includes instructions for all the findings needed for the projects shown. Make them yourself, or feel free to substitute purchased findings if you wish. Page references to correlating instructions and techniques are provided in each materials list.

Stitch Tip

While working an off-loom stitch, such as those described in this book, keep the needle in one hand (if you're right-handed then it would be your right hand) and the beaded piece in your other hand. When stringing on just a few seed beads at a time, use the needle as a pointer, and point and pierce beads so that they slide onto the needle. If you need to string on lots of beads at once, use the needle like a scoop in a shallow bowl of beads. Scoop with the needle and allow the beads to slide down the thread.

Diamond Beaded Earrings

Cylindrically shaped bugle beads are used in bead weaving, but there's no law saying they all must be made of glass. Heishi beads, available in a variety of gemstones, are a wonderful alternative to glass bugle beads. The following project instructions combine electric-green gaspeite heishi beads with environmentally friendly faux coral teardrop beads and coral-colored Japanese glass seed beads for a bright color contrast. For other adaptations, you can follow these same instructions and simply use different beads. Dark amethyst, transparent rainbow Japanese seed beads and white pearl-colored seed beads are used for another variation of this design (see page 49), which also includes a trocha shell teardrop and crystal dangle, as well as a crystal on the **beaded ear hook**. These diamond-shaped earrings incorporate the **ladder** and **Comanche** bead weaving stitches. They are finished off with a teardrop bead using the **basic fringe** technique. Finally, with a few inches of sterling wire you can make your own **basic ear hooks**.

MATERIALS

- ❯ fourteen 3 x 2-mm gaspeite heishi beads

- ❯ ten grams size 11 yellow-lined coral Japanese seed beads

- ❯ two 6 x 13-mm faux coral teardrop beads

- ❯ two sterling silver basic ear hooks (page 27)

- ❯ Silamide thread in natural and dusty rose

- ❯ size 12 beading needle

- ❯ round-nosed pliers

- ❯ scissors

1. Begin by threading the needle with natural-colored Silamide, and then use seven heishi beads to make one ladder of beads.

2. Repeat step 1 to make a second ladder, and use the **finishing thread** technique to finish off both the working thread and the thread tail before moving on to the next step.

3. Now thread the needle with dusty rose Silamide, and insert the needle through one heishi bead on either end of the ladder, leaving a 6" (15.2 cm) thread tail.

4. Next, use the **Comanche stitch** to attach the coral-colored seed beads to one side of the ladder.

5. Continue adding coral beads back and forth down the ladder until you have a total of five rows of beads. The last row should have two coral beads in it, and the thread will be positioned so it is coming out of the top of one of these two beads. You'll notice you now have made a triangle of beads.

6. String on four coral seed beads, and bring the needle down through the next bead in the last row so that you form a loop on the top of the triangle.

7. To make the loop a little stronger, insert the needle through the bottom of your first bead, and continue to thread it through the loop of beads until you come back out of the same bead in step 6.

8. After reinforcing the loop, continue to snake the needle and thread down through the triangle of seed beads until you come out on the other side of one end of the ladder.

9. Now you are ready to make another triangle of beads, to create the diamond shape. This time use **Comanche stitch** to make six rows of seed beads. The last row will have one bead on it, and the thread will come out of this last bead.

10. String on one coral teardrop bead and one coral-colored seed bead, use the **basic fringe** technique to make the teardrop into a dangle, and use the **finishing thread** technique to finish off the working thread and thread tail.

11. Repeat steps 3 through 10 for the second earring.

12. Use round-nosed pliers to gently open the **basic ear hook** (page xx) loop, slip the beaded loop at the top of one earring onto this wire loop, and then close the ear hook loop with the round-nosed pliers. Repeat this for the other earring. Trim off excess thread with scissors.

Beader's Tip *Always try to use thread that matches the color of the beads you chose as closely as possible. This will help make the thread virtually "disappear" throughout the design. Of course, this may not always be possible. If you have an unusual color or an odd combination of colors, try to use a neutral color of thread, such as beige or natural.*

Variation

Dark amethyst transparent rainbow Japanese seed beads and white pearl-colored seed beads are used in this variation.

Stitch Tip

When creating a beaded ladder piece, it's helpful to hold the beads you just attached between your index finger and thumb to keep the tension tight as you stitch your beads (the rungs of your ladder) together. Otherwise, you'll notice gaps appearing between the beads. If you still have gaps, you can sometimes tighten the tension by weaving the needle and thread back through the previously connected beads.

Diamond Beaded Necklace

A perfect match for the **Diamond Beaded Earrings**, this necklace completes the set. By including a longer ladder and making two small triangles of beads on one side and one large triangle of beads on the other side of the ladder section, this design matches the geometrical elements of the earrings. A third triangle of beads is stitched to the back so it just peeks out. Each of the three beaded "diamonds" has its own faux coral dangle, again using the **basic fringe** technique. More gaspeite heishi beads and coral-colored seed beads are combined with sterling silver daisy spacer beads for this double strand strap, which is finished off with sterling silver **bead tips**, **jump rings**, and a Bali-style clasp.

MATERIALS

- forty-two 3 x 2-mm gaspeite heishi beads
- 30 grams size 11 yellow-lined coral-colored Japanese seed beads
- three 6 x 13-mm faux coral teardrop beads
- forty 4-mm sterling silver daisy spacers
- two sterling silver bead tips
- two 5-mm sterling silver jump rings (page xx)
- one large sterling silver Bali-style S-hook clasp
- Silamide thread in natural and dusty rose
- two size 12 beading needles
- scissors
- jeweler's cement
- flat-nosed pliers
- corsage pin or beading awl
- round-nosed pliers

1. Thread a needle with natural-colored Silamide, and then use fifteen heishi beads to make one ladder of beads. Make another ladder of beads, but this time use only seven heishi beads, and set it aside for later.

2. Now thread the needle with dusty rose Silamide, and insert the needle through one heishi bead on either end of the ladder, leaving a 6" (15.2 cm) thread tail.

3. Use the **Comanche stitch** to attach the coral-colored seed beads to one side of the ladder.

4. Continue adding coral beads back and forth down the ladder until you have a total of eleven rows of beads. Your last row should have four coral beads in it.

5. If you have enough thread, snake the needle and thread down through the triangle of seed beads until you come out on the other side of one end of the ladder. If you need more thread, use the **finishing thread** technique and then the **adding thread** technique to add a longer piece of thread.

6. Now you are ready to make two bead triangles on the other side of the ladder. Start a row of **Comanche stitch** on the other side of the ladder, but stop weaving the first row after the seventh bead. Flip the piece around and continue back and forth until there are seven rows of seed beads. Your last row will have one bead on it, and the thread will come out of this last bead.

7. Using the **basic fringe** technique, create a dangle on the end with one coral teardrop bead and one coral-colored seed bead.

8. Snake the needle and thread up through the triangle of seed beads until you come out of the eighth heishi bead on the ladder.

9. Repeat steps 6 and 7 to make the other bead triangle, and use the **finishing thread**

technique to weave in all thread tails. Set this piece aside for later use.

10. Now you need to make half of a diamond piece with a dangle of faux coral. This is the beaded piece that you will stitch onto the back of the double triangle piece you just made. Using the seven-bead ladder piece you made in step 1, thread the needle with dusty rose Silamide, and insert the needle through one heishi bead on either end of the ladder, leaving a 6" (15.2 cm) thread tail.

11. Use the **Comanche stitch** to make six rows of seed beads. Your last row will have one bead on it, and, just as you did in step 7, use the **basic fringe** technique to add a faux coral teardrop bead to the end. Snake the thread back up through the triangle so that the needle comes out of one end of the ladder.

12. Now you are ready to attach the half-diamond piece to the double-diamond piece. Position the ladder of the half-diamond piece up against and in the middle of the ladder of the double diamond.

13. Hold the ladders against each other, and insert the needle through the thread that joins the fifth and sixth rungs of the double-diamond piece.

14. Continue to hold the ladders together, and insert the needle through the thread that joins the first and second rungs of the half-diamond piece.

15. Continue to stitch the two ladders together until you have the entire width of the half-diamond piece attached to the back and middle part of the double diamond, and then finish off the thread.

16. To attach a neck strap, use the **adding thread** technique, but instead of using a single thread thickness, make the thread double in thickness and about 24" (61 cm) in

length. Position the thread so that it comes out one of the last beads in the top row of the beaded diamond piece.

17. Once the thread is securely attached to the beaded diamond piece, use scissors to cut the doubled thread right at the point where it is attached to the needle (this will create two single pieces of thread), and attach a needle to each length of thread.

18. Insert both needles through one daisy bead, one heishi, and another daisy bead.

19. Next, thread seven coral-colored seed beads onto one thread and seven coral-colored seed beads onto the other thread.

20. Repeat steps 18 and 19 three times.

21. Repeat steps 18 and 19 two more times, but this time string on 14 coral-colored seed beads.

22. Repeat steps 18 and 19 three more times, but now string on 20 coral-colored seed beads, and then end the strap with one daisy bead, one heishi, and another daisy bead.

23. Use the jeweler's cement, flat-nosed pliers and corsage pin to finish the strand with a **bead tip**, and then use round-nosed pliers to curl the **bead tip** hook around the **jump ring**.

24. Repeat steps 16 through 23 for the other side of the strap, and attach the Bali-style S hook to both **jump rings**.

Beader's Tip

If you like the color of a bead but don't feel comfortable about its origins, explore the many "faux" alternatives available. Whether or not to use materials such as coral is a personal decision. If you don't like the idea of using materials that might harm the environment, there are plenty of options available so that you can get the look without the guilt. Faux coral is available from a number of bead suppliers and is normally made of glass, plastic, or resin.

Stitch Tip

When learning any new stitch, it's always important to make sure you have some quality beads and a good needle. Don't assume that since you're just playing around you don't need to use quality products. The opposite is actually true. Working with a bent needle or weaving with irregular-sized seed beads can cause aggravation, and when you're learning something new, you want to make it as easy as possible on yourself. You can always cut up your practice pieces and reuse your beads once you are comfortable with your newly acquired weaving stitch.

Fall Festival Bracelet

The fall-inspired color palette in this **free-form sculptural peyote** bracelet is collected from memories of falling leaves and evening sunsets. Don't expect to duplicate this exact bracelet design. That's not how this stitch technique works; each piece is meant to be unique. Instead, look in your own bead stash for similar com-ponents. Or better yet, take yourself on a little "fall palette" shopping spree at your favorite bead shop or online bead retailer. Once you get started constructing your own bead sculpture, allow the design to form organically. Remember: the best part of **free-form sculptural peyote** is that there is no wrong way to do it.

MATERIALS

> 10 grams each size 11 Japanese seed beads: translucent burgundy, translucent dark topaz, triangle bronze hex, and triangle gunmetal hex

> miscellaneous bead assortment: 4-mm bronze-colored pearls; garnet chips; bronze bugles; amber chips; leopard skin jasper chips; heart, rice, and round beads; 8-mm goldstone; oval citrine; diamond-shaped moonstone; rectangular brown glass

> gold-tone leaf button with back bale

> Silamide thread in gold

> size 12 beading needle

> scissors

1. Collect your palette of beads, making sure you have at least two to four types of seed beads to create the base of your bracelet.

2. Thread your needle and add a **stop bead** at the end, leaving about a 6" (15.2 cm) tail.

3. Using the seed beads selected, string on enough seed beads until they measure approximately 7 1/2" (19.1 cm) long.

4. Begin the **even count flat peyote stitch** with the seed beads (remembering that you can use any of the two to four types you selected in any order) until you have woven three or four rows of beads.

5. Now start weaving in other beads and mixing them with the seed beads as described in the **free-form sculptural peyote stitch** instructions.

6. Weave enough rows until the bracelet is approximately 1/4" (6 mm) wide.

7. Now make a **bead bridge** (as described in the **free-form sculptural peyote stitch** instructions), and make sure the space between the bridge of beads and the woven beads previously made is large enough for the leaf button to fit through. The easiest way to do this is to hold the stitching together with one

hand and use the other hand to slip the button through the space. If it's too big or too small, pull out the last stitch and add or subtract beads as necessary to make sure the space is the correct size.

8. It's a good idea to reinforce the hole that your button will fit through. To do this, insert the needle and thread through both the bottom side and the top (the bridge just made) a few times, making sure that the thread comes out at the end of the bridge.

9. Continue weaving beads in whatever order you want, going back and forth down the bracelet.

10. For some added detail, use the **basic fringe** technique to add short bead dangles here and there.

11. Weave the last row so that the needle and thread end up on the opposite end of the hole created in step 7.

12. Weave the needle back through the beads so the thread is positioned a few beads from the end and approximately in the middle of the bracelet. This way, the hole on the other end of the bracelet will align with the button.

Beader's Tip *Look for ways to include a variety of stone and crystal beads in your seed bead jewelry designs. Free-form sculptural peyote is great for this, but there are also design details such as amulet and necklace straps, fringe, and toggle clasps that provide opportunities for adding a little something unexpected into your woven jewelry pieces.*

13. Insert the needle through the bale on the back of the leaf button, bring it down through the beads in the bracelet, and then back up through the beads and bale again. Check to see how the button fits through the hole. If you'd prefer the button to be someplace else on the bracelet, take out the last few stitches and reposition it wherever you want.

14. Repeat step 13 until the button is securely attached to the bracelet.

15. Remove the stop bead, **finish off** the thread tail, and use scissors to trim off the excess thread.

Stitch Tip

When using the free-form sculptural peyote stitch, you'll be surprised how your design will seem to take on a life of its own. One moment, you'll love what's evolving in front of you, and the next moment doubts of "what the heck am I doing?!" will creep in. Although there's no guarantee that every single piece of jewelry you make will be a success, it's important to tune out those voices of doubt. If you give up too soon, then you won't know what might have come from this unique, creative process. Have some faith in yourself.

This free-from sculptural peyote bracelet with beaded toggle clasp was inspired by the sea. Materials used include white and blue freshwater pearls; royal blue teardrop crystals; Japanese seed beads in turquoise, royal blue, and white; size 6 matte blue beads; 4-mm blue cube glass beads; lapis lazuli chips and round beads; and Austrian bicone-shaped crystals in clear and blue.

Artist: Tammy Powley

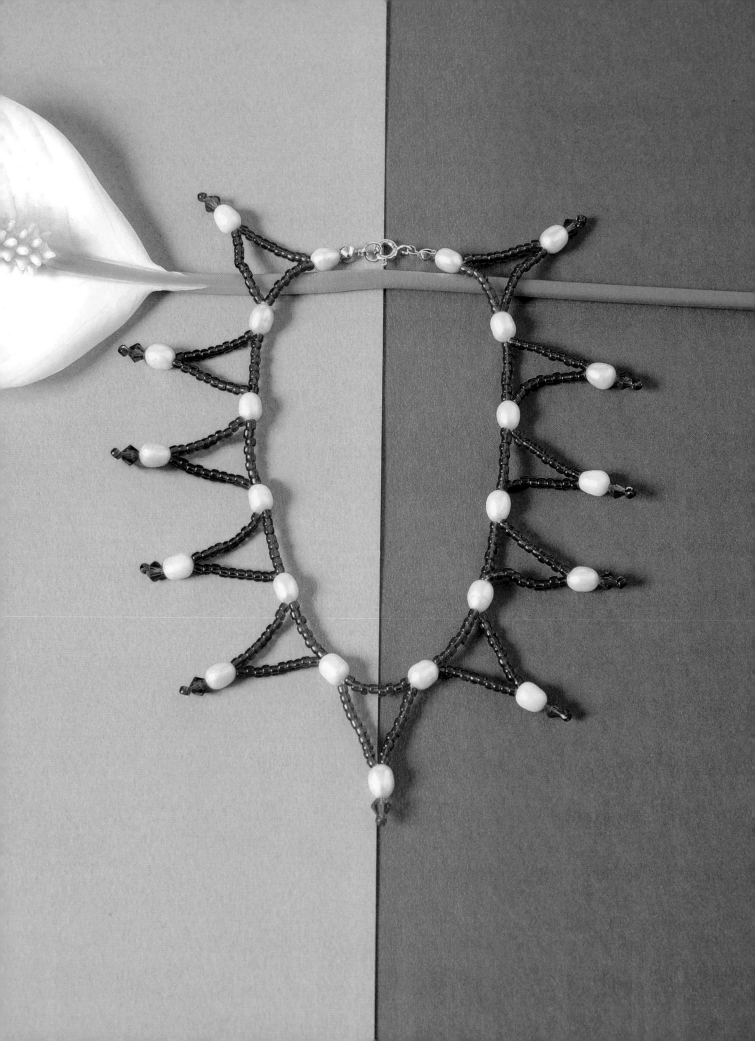

Lacy Emerald Anklet

What could be daintier than a little lace around the ankle? The **single thread netting** stitch is a perfect way to accomplish the look of lace. Add some extra romance to your design with pearls and sparkling crystal bicone beads. Sea foam-colored pearls and emerald Swarovski crystals combine with dark green seed beads in this super-easy and versatile project. Follow the directions exactly and make an anklet, or, if you prefer, make the piece smaller for a bracelet or larger to create a necklace.

MATERIALS

- twenty-three 4-mm light green pearls

- 10 grams size 11 translucent emerald Japanese seed beads

- eleven 4-mm bicone emerald-colored Swarovski crystals

- two sterling silver bead tips

- one sterling silver 4-mm jump ring (page 27)

- one sterling silver 4.5-mm spring ring clasp

- Silamide thread in kelly green

- two size 12 beading needles

- scissors

- jeweler's cement

- flat-nosed pliers

- one corsage pin or beading awl

- pin cushion

- round-nosed pliers

1. First, you need to make a base row, including an extra thread for the netting. (Your base row is a double thickness of thread, and the extra netting thread is a single thickness.) Thread one needle with a few feet of thread, and pull the thread to double its thickness. Thread a second needle with a few feet of thread, and use the jeweler's cement, flat-nosed pliers, and corsage pin to attach one **bead tip** to the ends of all these threads.

2. Pull the netting thread aside so that it is out of the way, and secure the needle in a safe place, such as a pin cushion.

3. On the doubled thread, string on one pearl and eight seed beads. Continue to alternate this pattern (one pearl, eight seed beads) until you end the pattern with a total of twelve pearls.

4. Finish the end of the doubled thread (leaving the netting thread free) with another **bead tip**.

5. You are ready to start working with the remaining thread. Insert the needle through the first pearl on the base row.

6. Use the **single thread netting technique with dangle** to stitch around the anklet. The first part of each dangle requires ten seed beads, one pearl, one crystal, and one seed bead. The second side of the dangle segment requires ten seed beads.

7. Thread the needle through the second pearl on the base row, and continue around the anklet until you have a total of ten dangle segments.

8. Make one more dangle segment (for a total of eleven), and insert the needle through the last pearl on the base row. The thread should be positioned right before the bead tip.

9. Use the netting thread to make an overhand knot right past the pearl and against the base row thread. (If necessary, use a corsage pin to help with pushing the knot against the base row thread.)

Beader's Tip *Pearl beads are wonderful to include in your seed bead jewelry. Thanks to new jewelry technology, pearls are now available in a huge assortment of colors and shapes. Look for colors that coordinate with your favorite seed beads and crystals. Pearls often have small holes, so they are easy to combine into woven seed bead designs. Use them for accents, in fringe, or as bead stations throughout your woven beaded jewelry.*

10. Now thread the needle back through the last pearl in the direction you just came from, and continue to snake the needle and thread through the base row beads for a few inches.

11. Use the **finishing thread** technique to secure and finish off the netting thread.

12. Finally, use round-nosed pliers to curl the hook on one **bead tip** around a **jump ring**, and then repeat this to attach a spring ring clasp to the other **bead tip**.

Stitch Tip

Learning a new stitch can be frustrating at times, but there are a few methods that can help ensure success. First, use the suggested beads or other materials described in the instructions. For example, if Delica beads are suggested, don't try to use Czech seed beads instead. Start with just a few beads and a little thread to get an understanding of a stitch before jumping into a new jewelry project. Then, try to follow the written and illustrated instructions simultaneously, moving back and forth from the written words to the illustrations as you follow with the beads and thread in hand. Finally, expect a few false starts that may require you to pull apart your practice piece and start over.

This combination stitch bracelet consists of earthy-green seed beads woven with stations of light green pearls. The artist used the netting stitch for part of the bracelet, and then allowed the ends of the netting to attach to peyote bead sections.

Artist: Jennifer Shibona

Shades of Blue Necklace

Just about everyone looks good wearing the color blue, and there are so many shade variations to use in jewelry making. This necklace incorporates two shades of blue for a color-contrast effect: a light, bright blue turquoise and a dark, rich royal blue. Accents of button-shaped pearls and sterling silver daisy spacer beads frame the design. **Single thread netting stitch** is one of the easiest weaving stitches to learn, and it's very versatile. Two strands of netting are attached to a single base row of beads in this necklace. It also includes a sterling silver clasp you can make yourself using the **quadruple loop eye** and **triple loop clasp** instructions located in the Seed Bead and Related Jewelry Techniques section of this book. The finished piece measures approximately 18 inches (45.7 cm) in length and rests just below the collarbone.

MATERIALS

- 20 grams size 11 translucent turquoise-blue Japanese seed beads

- twenty-three 4-mm white button pearls

- eight 6-mm turquoise-blue Czech crystals

- 20 grams size 11 translucent royal blue Japanese seed beads

- seven 10 x 8-mm cobalt blue teardrop Czech crystals

- twenty-three 4-mm sterling silver daisy spacer beads

- two sterling silver bead tips

- one sterling silver quadruple loop eye (page 30)

- one sterling silver triple loop hook (page 30)

- Silamide thread in aqua

- two size 12 beading needles

- jeweler's cement

- flat-nosed pliers

- corsage pin or beading awl

- pin cushion

- round-nosed pliers

- scissors

1. First, you need to make the base row, and include an extra thread for the netting. Your base row is a double thickness of thread, and the extra netting thread is a single thickness. Thread one needle with approximately 4' (122 cm) of thread, and pull the thread to double its thickness. Thread a second needle with a few feet of thread, and use the jeweler's cement, flat-nosed pliers, and corsage pin to attach one **bead tip** to the ends of all the threads.

2. Pull the netting thread aside so that it is out of the way, and secure the needle in a safe place, such as a pin cushion.

3. On your doubled thread, string on twenty turquoise seed beads.

4. Then string on the following bead pattern: one pearl, one daisy spacer, one turquoise crystal, one daisy spacer, and another pearl bead.

5. Now string on fifteen royal blue seed beads, and repeat the bead pattern from the previous step (pearl, daisy, crystal, daisy, pearl).

6. String on fifteen turquoise seed beads, and repeat the bead pattern from step 4.

7. Continue to alternate fifteen royal blue seed beads, the bead pattern, and fifteen turquoise seed beads and the bead pattern five more times, making sure you end with the bead pattern (pearl, daisy, crystal, daisy, pearl).

8. String on twenty turquoise seed beads, and finish the end of the doubled thread (leaving the netting thread free) with another **bead tip**.

9. You are ready to start working with the remaining thread. Thread the needle through the seed beads and bead pattern section so that the thread comes out of a pearl bead.

Beader's Tip

*When using the netting stitch for the first time, it's helpful to have either a large bead or stations of beads (such as the bead pattern used in the **Shades of Blue Necklace project**) positioned symmetrically on the base row of the jewelry piece. For example, a base row might alternate ten seed beads, one crystal bead, ten seed beads, and one crystal bead. This helps determine where each area of netting begins and ends. If you prefer to use all seed beads and not include larger crystal, pearl, or gemstone beads in a netted design, another alternative is to use a different color seed bead to help mark each area of netting.*

Keep an open mind when it comes to learning different types of bead weaving stitches. One element of bead weaving art is to take an existing stitch or pattern and build on it to make variations. This is one way that jewelry designers grow creatively, and it also brings new ideas and new possibilities to the genre. If every jewelry maker created jewelry the exact same way, there would never be anything new to learn. No art form remains stagnant.

10. Use the **single thread netting with dangle** technique to stitch around the necklace. The first part of each dangle requires ten royal blue seed beads, one pearl, one daisy spacer, one teardrop bead, and one royal blue seed bead. The second side of the dangle section requires ten turquoise seed beads.

11. Thread the needle through the second bead pattern section on the base row, so that the thread comes out of the second pearl bead, and continue around until you have a total of seven dangle segments.

12. Now it's time to make the second row of the necklace. This stitch is **single thread netting without dangles**. The thread should be positioned so that it is coming out of the last pearl on the necklace. Insert the needle through the turquoise seed bead just past the pearl, and then, heading in the opposite direction and working your way back down the necklace for a second time, insert the needle back into the pearl. (The turquoise seed bead is working as an anchor here, and because the thread is the same color, it will be barely visible.)

13. Continue to snake the needle and thread back through the next fifteen royal blue seed beads, and then down through the first five turquoise beads in the dangle previously made.

14. String on twenty royal blue seed beads, and then insert the needle up through the next dangle section, starting at the fifth royal blue seed bead.

15. Continue to snake the needle and thread up through the dangle and then down the base row of the necklace.

16. Continue this second row of netting, alternating turquoise seed beads and royal blue seed beads, until you reach the last dangle.

17. Snake the needle and thread up to the necklace's base row and past the last bead pattern section.

18. Use the **finishing thread** technique to secure and finish off the netting thread.

19. Finally, use round-nosed pliers to curl the hook on one **bead tip** around the **quadruple loop eye**, and then repeat this to attach a **triple loop hook** to the other **bead tip**.

Hearty Fringe Earrings

These fringe earrings are a classic design just about every bead weaver learns. They combine the **ladder** and **Comanche stitches** and then finish off with the **basic fringe** technique. Fringe is a great way to include other beads besides seed beads, and for this project, rose quartz heart-shaped beads dangle from each piece of fringe. To bring the design together, the **beaded ear hooks** also include heart-shaped bead details. Whether you need some ladder and Comanche stitch practice or you're in the mood for a quick and easy project, this is a fun earring design. For a different look, just change the beads and dangle elements. In the brilliant blue fringe earrings pictured on page 69, light and dark blue beads are combined with pale blue bugle beads, and the dangles are packed full of bicone and teardrop-shaped crystal beads for added sparkle.

MATERIALS

- twenty ½" (1.3 cm) hematite-colored bugle beads

- 10 grams size 11 opaque cream-colored Japanese seed beads

- ten 4-mm rose quartz heart-shaped beads

- two sterling silver beaded ear hooks (page 28), each with a rose quartz heart-shaped bead

- Silamide thread in natural

- size 12 beading needle

- scissors

- round-nosed pliers

1. After threading the needle, use the **ladder stitch** to connect five bugle beads together, remembering to leave about a 6" (15.2 cm) thread tail.

2. Next, bring the needle up through one bugle bead on the end of the ladder section previously stitched, and use the **Comanche stitch** to weave three rows of seed beads. The last row should have two seed beads in it, with the thread coming out of one of these two beads.

3. String on six seed beads, and bring the needle down through the next bead in the last row to form a loop.

4. To make the loop a little stronger, insert the needle through the bottom of the first bead, and continue to thread it through the loop of beads until you come back out of the same bead in step 2.

5. After reinforcing the loop, continue to snake the needle and thread down through the seed beads until you come out on the other side of one end of your ladder.

6. String on three seed beads, one bugle, two seed beads, one rose quartz heart-shaped bead (with the point of the heart facing away from you), and one seed bead.

7. Use the **basic fringe** technique to bring the needle and thread up and then down through the next bugle bead.

8. String on four seed beads, one bugle, three seed beads, one rose quartz heart-shaped bead, and one seed bead.

9. Use the **basic fringe** technique to bring the needle and thread up and then down through the next bugle bead.

10. Repeats steps 6 and 7; steps 8 and 9; and then steps 6 and 7 again to complete the fringe.

11. Use the **finishing thread** technique to finish off the working thread and thread tail.

12. Repeat steps 1 through 11 to make a second earring.

13. Use round-nosed pliers to gently open the **beaded ear hook** loop, slip the beaded loop at the top of one earring onto this wire loop, and then close the ear hook loop again with round-nosed pliers. Repeat this for the other earring.

Beader's Tip *Not all beads will have large enough holes to fit on 20-gauge wire. It's always a good idea to double-check that the beads you plan to include on your ear hooks will fit before deciding to include them in other areas of a jewelry design. Also, be careful of gemstone bead shapes such as stars and hearts. They often have flaws, such as crookedly drilled holes. Again, double-check the quality of the beads you plan to use in a design before starting to weave a piece together.*

Variation

Dark and light blue beads are combined with pale blue bugle beads and crystal dangles.

In this piece, seed beads in three shades of purple are woven to create ladder and netting stitches. Netting loops are accented with light amethyst-colored crystals, as is the fringe, which also includes faceted amethyst briolette gemstones. The choker ends are finished with bead loops and a gold-filled S-hook clasp.

Artist: Tammy Powley

Bronze and Gold Multistrand Necklace

This necklace features nine strands of beads brimming over with crystals, metal, glass, stones, and pearls. All the selected beads are derived from a metallic color palette: gold, brass, copper, and silver. You only need to know two stitches: **ladder** and **Comanche**. This is a chance to let your creative juices flow. Mix up your beads. Use lots of different shapes, shades, and textures to add depth to the design. The bead strands don't even need to be exactly the same length as long as they are each around 15 to 16 inches (38.1 to 40.6 cm). When you wear it, let the strands fall where they may, or twist them a little for a chunkier look.

MATERIALS

- eighteen 1/4" (6 mm) rainbow-root-beer-colored bugle beads

- 40 grams size 11 translucent amber-colored Japanese seed beads

- 10 grams size 11 round bronze-colored Czech seed beads

- 10 grams size 11 round silver-lined Japanese seed beads

- one 10-mm round gold-colored AB crystal bead

- miscellaneous bead assortment: goldstone round and chip beads; bronze-colored potato and oval pearls; gold-colored rectangular pearls; oval and round citrine; amber chips; 4-mm, 6-mm, and 8-mm goldstone; 4-mm and 8-mm tiger's-eye; 4-mm round, heart-shaped, and chip leopard skin jasper; 4-mm bicone clear AB crystals; 6-mm amber-colored round crystals; 4-mm bicone amber-colored crystals;

6-mm and 4-mm light topaz-colored glass beads; root beer-colored bugle beads; vintage crystals; metallic faceted gold-colored Czech crystals; and an assortment of copper and sterling silver daisy spacers and gold-vermeil beads

- Silamide thread in gold

- size 12 beading needle

- scissors

1. Thread the needle with about 3' (91.4 cm) of thread, take nine bugle beads, and connect them using the **ladder stitch**.

2. Next, use the amber-colored seed beads and the **Comanche stitch** to make two rows of beads on top of the ladder piece.

3. Continue to use the **Comanche stitch** for the following rows: use round bronze-colored Czech seed beads for row 3; silver-lined Japanese seed beads for row 4; round bronze-colored Czech seed beads for row 5; and amber-colored Japanese seed beads for rows 6, 7, and 8.

4. String on seven amber-colored beads, one 10-mm round gold-colored AB crystal, and one amber-colored bead.

5. Follow the **beaded toggles** and **finishing thread** instructions to complete this bead component, and set it aside for later.

6. Repeat steps 1 through 3 above, except stop at row 7 so that there are two amber-colored beads in the last row.

7. String on twenty-four amber-colored beads, and follow the **beaded toggles** and **finishing thread** instructions to complete this bead component.

8. At this point, you should have two beaded components, so you are now ready to connect these with nine strands of beads. Thread 6' (1.8 m) of thread onto the needle. For the rest of the necklace, you will need a lot of thread, so if you can handle working with longer than 6' (1.8 m), go ahead. If not, you will just need to use the **adding thread** technique more often.

9. Use the **adding thread** technique to add the thread onto one of the beaded components previously made, making sure that the thread comes out one end of one ladder.

Beader's Tip

Most beaders will discover they lean toward certain color selections. Although it's nice to try out other colors once in a while, returning to the same colors again and again can sometimes be a good thing when you want to make a piece of jewelry that uses one color palette. More than likely, you already have most of the beads you need because you've been collecting beads in your favorite colors for a while. If you don't have a large enough bead stash yet, consider some of the bead mixes offered by beading suppliers. Many sell prepackaged bead collections in compatible color palettes that include an assortment of shapes and styles.

10. Begin to string on the assortment of beads. The amber-colored beads are the primary beads, but also use the other seed beads to separate the larger accent beads; add a few seed beads, add an accent bead, add a few seed beads, and add an accent bead. Continue this until there are about 15" (38.1 cm) of beads.

11. Now thread the needle through the corresponding bugle bead on the other end and up through the seed bead positioned above the bugle.

12. To reinforce each necklace strand at this stage, you need to secure the thread and bring it back through the strand. The thread is coming out of the top of the first seed bead on the first row of **Comanche stitch**. Insert the needle in the thread above this bead (also called a bridge thread), tie an overhand knot with the thread, and then insert it back down through the seed bead and bugle bead.

13. Continue to snake the needle back through the strand you just strung, a few beads at a time, until you get to the other end. (Pay extra careful attention here so that you don't accidentally skip a bead.)

14. When you meet up with the other bead component, bring the needle up through the bugle bead, and then down through the next bugle bead.

15. Continue to repeat steps 10 through 14 for all other strands, **adding** and **finishing threads** as necessary until you have completed all nine strands.

Radiant Zircon Earrings

Zircon is a silicate mineral, and though its color range includes yellow, brown, and violet, the most well known is blue zircon. Therefore, the term *zircon* also refers to a light blue/green shade of blue. In this earring design, large bicone crystals, the color of blue zircon, enhance **beaded ear hooks** and dangle from a matching rectangle of Delica seed beads woven together using the **square stitch**. The variation earrings pictured on page 77 utilize the same instructions but different beads. Silver Delicas make up the center beaded rectangle and are accented with copper- and maroon-colored seed beads. A 6-mm gold Czech crystal bead accents the wire **ear hooks**.

MATERIALS

- ❯ 5 grams forest green–lined Delica beads

- ❯ two 6-mm zircon-colored bicone crystal beads

- ❯ two gold-filled beaded ear hooks (page 28), each with a 6-mm zircon-colored bicone crystal bead

- ❯ Silamide thread in aqua

- ❯ size 12 beading needle

- ❯ round-nosed pliers

- ❯ scissors

1. Thread the needle, and use **the four-bead-wide square stitch** instructions to create a rectangular beaded section that is four Delica beads wide and ten Delica beads long. Make sure you leave a 12" (30.5 cm) thread tail for later use.

2. After making the rectangular beaded section, the working thread should be positioned at one end of the last four-wide row of beads. String ten Delica beads onto the thread.

3. Insert the needle through the last bead on the other side of the bead row to form a loop at the top of the rectangle.

4. To reinforce the loop, insert the needle through the last row, and up through the bead loop again.

5. Use the **finishing thread** technique to finish off the working thread.

6. Attach the needle to the tail, and string on four Delica beads, one zircon-colored crystal, and four more Delica beads.

7. Insert the needle through the last bead on the other side of the bead row to form a loop at the bottom of the rectangle.

8. Reinforce the loop as described in step 4, and use the **finishing thread** technique to finish off the thread tail.

9. Repeat steps 1 through 8 for a second earring.

10. Slightly open the loop on one **beaded ear hook** with round-nosed pliers, slip on the earring's beaded loop, and use round-nosed pliers to close the wire around the beaded loop. Repeat this for the other earring.

Beader's Tip *Descriptive names for bead colors don't always do justice to the actual color of the beads. Catalog photographs and website images are usually fairly close to showing a bead's true color, but be prepared for a bead to be a little lighter or darker in color when ordering beads that you can't see "in person" before purchasing. If a bead looks nothing like what you expected when you ordered it, check the vendor's return policy. Most will let you return items within ten days of purchase.*

Variation

Silver Delicas make up the center beaded rectangle accented with copper maroon and crystal beads.

Stitch Tip

In addition to the size of a bead's hole, the size of the needle and thread are also important considerations when bead weaving. Thinner thread and thinner needles will allow you to use beads with smaller holes. It's always a good idea to test out a needle and thread with the beads you plan to use before starting a project. This is especially important if a stitch requires that you make multiple passes through a bead. However, if you get stuck in a situation where you need to pass your needle through a bead again but it just doesn't fit, try changing out your current needle with a thinner one. It may give you the extra room you need to pass through the bead's hole.

Dainty Delica Bracelet

Tiny crystals surround gemstones in flower-motif bead blossoms positioned down the length of this delicate **square stitch** and **beaded toggle** bracelet. Here, cream-colored Delicas create a backdrop to highlight the amethyst crystals and black onyx beads. Once you make this bracelet, you'll want to make a few more in different colors to wear side by side on your wrist.

Bead weaver Ruth Neese did exactly that, illustrating that you can never have too many **square stitch beaded toggle** bracelets. One in pink, one in purple, and one in green (see page 81), these bracelets look great worn together or separately. Each is made of color-coordinating Delica beads, crystals, and gemstones, just like the bracelet featured in this project.

MATERIALS

- ❯ 5 grams opaque cream-colored Delica beads
- ❯ sixteen 3-mm light amethyst bicone crystal beads
- ❯ five 4-mm black onyx beads
- ❯ Silamide thread in natural
- ❯ size 12 beading needle
- ❯ scissors

1. Thread the needle and make sure you leave a 12" (30.5 cm) tail before starting the stitch.

2. Use the **square stitch** instructions to create a rectangular beaded section that is two Delica beads wide and twenty Delica beads long.

3. String on one crystal bead, one onyx bead, and another crystal bead, and insert the needle down and through the last row of **square stitch** beads.

4. Insert the needle back up through the next crystal and the onyx bead.

5. String on one crystal bead, two Delicas, and one crystal bead.

6. Insert the needle through the onyx bead, then the next crystal bead, and through the two Delica beads.

7. Continue the **square stitch**, using the two Delica beads previous strung as the first row, to make another rectangular beaded section that is two Delica beads wide and twenty Delica beads long.

8. Repeat steps 3 through 7 until there are a total of five rectangular beaded sections alternating with four crystal and onyx sections. At this point, the working thread should be positioned so that it is coming out of the last row of Delica **square stitch** beads.

9. String on ten Delica beads, and use the **beaded toggle** instructions to make the toggle loop of the clasp.

10. Use the **finishing thread** technique to finish off the working thread, and then attach the needle to the thread tail on the other end of the bracelet.

11. Thread on four Delicas, one onyx bead, and one Delica, and use the **beaded toggle** instructions to make the other side of the toggle clasp.

12. Use the **finishing thread** technique to finish off the remaining thread.

Beader's Tip *Beaded toggles are a good way to integrate gemstones, crystals, and pearl beads into a seed bead design. Before making and finishing off a beaded toggle for the first time, it's always a good idea to check that the loop will fit around the selected toggle bead. Make a sample loop of beads, and try to push the bead selected for the toggle through the loop a few times. Once you're confident that it fits, reinforce the loop and bead sections by inserting the needle back through a few times, and then finish off any remaining threads.*

Variation

Dark and light blue beads are combined with pale blue bugle beads and crystal dangles.
Artist: Ruth Neese

Stitch Tip

No matter which stitches are used for a design, many woven jewelry pieces require additional threads to be added. Although some beaders prefer to stick with using knots alone to add new threads, some also like to add a dab of glue or clear fingernail polish to help secure the knots. There's nothing wrong with using glue. Just be careful when doing so, because glue or polish can clog up the hole in a bead and make it impossible to insert a needle through. If you choose to use glue, do so only after all the weaving is finished.

Petite Pearl Peyote Amulet

Amulets are a favorite jewelry design among bead weavers. Consisting of a small beaded pouch with an attached strap, amulets are perfect for storing personal talismans: a lucky coin, a lock of hair, or a fortune cookie message. Experienced bead weavers often weave very elaborate amulets, some including intricate designs and patterns. However, the less experienced weaver can still create beautiful amulets by selecting the right combination of beads. This petite amulet includes shades of pink and mixes pearls and rose quartz with light pink Delica beads. A gold-filled **S-hook clasp** connects the necklace straps. The **even count flat peyote** amulet is embellished with **basic fringe** strands on the sides and **swag fringe** at the bottom.

MATERIALS

- 20 grams peach-lined AB Delica beads

- nine 3- or 4-mm side-drilled light pink pearls

- fifteen 3- or 4-mm light pink button pearls

- forty-four 4-mm rose quartz beads

- one gold-filled S-hook clasp (page 26)

- Silamide thread in rose

- size 12 beading needle

- scissors

1. Thread the needle, attach a **stop bead**, leaving about a 6" (15.2 cm) tail, and string on twenty-four Delica beads.

2. Using the **even count flat peyote** instructions, continue to weave with Delica beads until the piece is approximately 2" (5.1 cm) wide and 1¼" (3.1 cm) long, **adding thread** as needed.

3. Remove the **stop bead**, and fold the piece in half so that the edges meet. You'll notice that the edges on both sides look similar to the teeth on a zipper, so that where a bead sticks out on one side there is an indent for it on the other side. Hold the sides up next to each other, and lock the teeth in place.

4. Continue to hold the beaded peyote piece, locking the teeth together, and insert the needle up through the bottom of the bead closest to the needle.

5. Connect both sides by threading the needle up through the teeth (the beads sticking out) so you zigzag back and forth.

6. To help reinforce the amulet, repeat the zigzag stitching back down in the opposite direction. At this point, you will have a tube-shaped beaded piece that is 1" (2.5 cm) wide.

7. Use the **finishing thread** technique to weave the tail in.

8. To close the bottom of the tube, select one end of the tube, and hold both sides together so that the beads line up next to each other. They will not look like zipper teeth this time, but instead will be two straight lines of beads, with their holes pointing toward you.

9. Starting at one end of the tube, use the **adding thread** technique to weave in a new working thread, positioning it so that it exits from one bead on the end. You can pick either of the two straight lines of beads to begin stitching the bottom closed; just make sure you are at the end of whichever line of beads you select.

Beader's Tip *Pearls are available in a large range of shapes and sizes, from traditional round pearls to square and even rectangle shapes. Use different shapes and sizes to create dimension and interest in your woven designs. Most pearls have fairly small holes, so they work well with seed beads because they both require thin needles. Just make sure you double-check that the needle can fit through the pearls before starting a project. However, you can also switch to a smaller needle, if necessary.*

*When learning the **peyote stitch** for the first time, it's worth a little extra money to purchase Delicas or, at the very least, Japanese seed beads. Otherwise, trying to use beads that may not be preciously cut can cause a lot of frustration. Also, avoid using matte-finished beads because they tend to move around a lot while weaving. Once you feel comfortable with the **peyote stitch**, it will be easier to handle matte or even Czech seed beads while weaving this stitch.*

10. Insert the needle down through the bead directly opposite of the bead where the working thread exits.

11. Bring the needle down through the top of the bead next to it.

12. Repeat steps 10 and 11, moving back and forth from one line of beads to the other, until the bottom of the tube is closed, and then finish off the thread.

13. Next, add a strap to both sides of the top of the tube (the only part that is now open) by **adding thread** and making sure the thread comes out on one end of the top of the amulet tube.

14. String on three Delicas and one rose quartz bead.

15. Repeat the above bead pattern in step14.

16. String on three Delicas, one button pearl, one rose quartz bead, and one button pearl.

17. Repeat the bead pattern in step 14 five times, and then repeat step 16 one time.

18. Repeat step 14 four times, step 16 once, and step 14 eight times.

19. Repeat steps 13 through 18 for the other side of the strap.

20. To include some embellishments, use the **adding thread** and then the **basic fringe** technique to attach two pieces of fringe next to the straps. Use five Delicas and end with one side-drilled pearl for the shorter fringe, and seven Delicas and end with one side-drilled pearl for the longer fringe. Add a short and long fringe piece to either side of the amulet.

21. For the first **swag fringe** embellishment at the bottom of the amulet, string on three Delicas, one pearl button, two Delicas, one pearl button, two Delicas, one pearl button, and three Delicas.

22. For the second swag fringe, string on three Delicas, one side-drilled pearl, one Delica, and one side-drilled pearl, and continue alternating until there is a total of five side-drilled pearls. End with three Delicas.

23. Attach the **S-hook clasp** to both loops at the top of the amulet strap.

Midnight Vintage Necklace

Space-age technology is given a vintage look with jet-black aurora borealis (AB) Czech crystal beads in this elegant cabochon necklace. The cabochon is made from dichroic glass, which was originally developed by aerospace engineers. Eventually, artisans discovered this new material and began using it in jewelry as well as other glass-related artwork. Jet crystals were popular during the Victorian era because Queen Victoria made it vogue to wear black. The necklace strap is glued to the back of the **bead embroidery** cabochon and then concealed with black suede. The ends of the strap are finished with **crimp beads** and a sterling silver **triple loop hook** and **quadruple loop eye** clasp.

MATERIALS

- ½" x ¾" (1.3 x 1.9 cm) dichroic glass cabochon

- 20 grams size 11 opaque black Japanese seed beads

- eight 8 x 6-mm teardrop jet AB Czech crystal beads

- four 6-mm cube Montana blue Swarovski crystal beads

- twenty-eight 4-mm jet AB Czech crystal beads

- two 2 x 2-mm sterling silver crimp beads

- one sterling silver quadruple loop eye (page 30)

- sterling silver triple loop hook (page 30)

- 24" (61 cm) size .014 beading wire

- Silamide thread in black

- 1" x 1" (2.5 x 2.5 cm) Stiff Stuff interfacing

- 1" x 1" (2.5 x 2.5 cm) black suede

- E6000 or tacky glue

- size 12 beading needle

- scissors

- crimping pliers

- wire cutters

1. Using E6000, glue the back of the glass cabochon to the interfacing and allow it to dry before proceeding.

2. Thread the needle, and use the **bead embroidery couching** instructions and black Japanese seed beads to stitch two rows around the cabochon.

3. Follow this with one row of **bead embroidery picot stitch**, using three seed beads for each stitch of picot edging.

4. With scissors, carefully trim off excess interfacing around the cabochon.

5. Now trim the piece of suede so that it is about 1/8" (3 mm) larger than the interfacing.

6. Locate the center of the beading wire, and glue this to the back of the interfacing, approximately 1/4" (6 mm) from the top of the cabochon. Be careful not to get the glue too close to the edges. Then glue the suede over the beading wire and interfacing, sandwiching the beading wire between the interfacing and the suede.

7. Gently press the suede against the cabochon, allow it to dry thoroughly, and then use a needle and thread to **whipstitch** around the suede so that it completely covers the interfacing.

8. Now you are ready to add beads to either side of the necklace strap. On one side, string on three black seed beads, one teardrop crystal (narrow end pointing away from the cabochon), one seed bead, one blue crystal cube, another seed bead, and one teardrop crystal (narrow end pointing toward the cabochon).

9. String on three seed beads, one 4-mm crystal bead, three seed beads, and another 4-mm crystal bead.

10. Repeat step 8.

11. To finish the beads on this side of the strap, continue to alternate three seed beads and one 4-mm crystal bead until you have added twelve more 4-mm crystal beads. Make sure you end with a 4-mm crystal.

12. Finish the end with a **crimp bead**, making sure to add on the **quadruple loop eye** before closing the crimp bead with crimping pliers.

13. Repeat steps 8 through 11 for the other side of the necklace strap.

14. Complete the necklace with a **crimp bead** and a **triple loop hook**.

Beader's Tip *The term* cabochon, *often shortened to "cab," refers to a jewelry component that is flat on one side and domed on the other. Cabochons come in a lot of different shapes, and though stone cabochons are probably the first type most jewelry makers think about, they can also be made of glass, porcelain, or even resin. Almost anything that is flat on one side can be glued to interfacing and beaded around.*

If you're interested in experimenting with beaded embroidery, start by learning some of the basics of embroidery without the beads. Many of the concepts and stitches transfer well to beadwork. Familiar embroidery stitches such as cross-stitch, chain stitch, and buttonhole stitch can all be combined with beads. You can even use embroidery canvas with beaded embroidery and literally paint a picture with your beads.

This outstanding beaded embroidery piece features a serpentine cabochon. It includes multiple shades of green and copper seed beads in the strap and picot edging, along with tourmaline gemstones and crystals in the basic fringe.

Artist: Ruth Neese

Golden Cabochon Necklace

A gemstone cabochon first starts out as a rock slab before the shaping process begins. This requires a cabochon machine, which is made up of numerous diamond wheels, each serving a different purpose to cut, shape, and polish the finished cabochon. In this **beaded embroidery** cabochon necklace, the focal piece is a mustard-colored jasper stone.

Sparkling crystals in golds and greens form a Y, and the cabochon hangs from the center. A few vintage crystals, available at most bead stores and through many online vendors, are interspersed between contemporary crystals. The straps are finished off with **crimp beads** and a gold-filled **quadruple loop eye** and **triple loop hook**.

MATERIALS

- one 24-mm mustard-colored round jasper cabochon

- 10 grams size 11 metallic bronze Czech seed beads

- 10 grams size 11 rainbow olive Japanese seed beads

- 10 grams size 11 metallic gold Japanese seed beads

- forty size 6 olive-colored seed beads

- twenty 6-mm smoky topaz-colored AB Swarovski crystals

- ten 8-mm gold-colored vintage crystals

- twenty 4-mm light topaz–colored crystals

- eight 4-mm olivine Swarovski crystals

- three gold-filled 2x2-mm crimp beads

- one gold-filled quadruple loop eye (page 30)

- one gold-filled triple loop hook (page 30)

- 30" (76.2 cm) size .014 beading wire

- Silamide thread in gold

- 2" x 2" (5.1 x 5.1 cm) Stiff Stuff interfacing

- 2" x 2" (5.1 x 5.1 cm) light tan suede

- E6000 or tacky glue

- size 12 beading needle

- scissors

- crimping pliers

- wire cutters

1. Glue the cabochon onto a piece of interfacing and allow it to dry before proceeding.

2. Thread the needle, and stitch once around the cabochon with the metallic bronze seed beads using the **embroidery couching** instructions.

3. Repeat step 2 with the rainbow olive seed beads.

4. Repeat step 2 with the metallic gold seed beads, and **finish off** the working thread.

5. With scissors, carefully trim off the excess interfacing around the beaded cabochon.

6. Trim the piece of suede so that is about $^1/_8$" (3 mm) larger than the interfacing.

7. Fold the beading wire in half, insert one **crimp bead** onto both ends of the wire, and push the crimp bead down to about 1" (2.5 cm) from the end.

8. Use crimping pliers to close the **crimp bead** around the doubled beading wire. This will create a small circle at the end of the beading wire.

9. Squeeze some glue onto the back of the cabochon. Be careful not to get glue too close to the edges.

10. Position the circle end of the beading wire on the back of the cabochon, making sure the **crimp bead** doesn't show past the beads around the cabochon.

11. Place the suede circle on the back of the cabochon, sandwiching the beading wire in between the cabochon and the suede.

12. Gently press the suede against the cabochon and allow it to dry before continuing.

13. Use a needle and thread to **whipstitch** around the suede so that it completely covers the interfacing.

14. Now it's time to make the Y-style strap. Holding both beading wire pieces together, string on one size 6 olive seed bead, one smoky topaz crystal, and another olive bead. From now on, this set of beads will be referred to as Pattern A.

15. String on one 8-mm gold crystal, and one Pattern A bead set.

16. At this point, separate the two bead wire strands and continue to string beads onto each individual strand.

17. On one strand, string on one 4-mm light topaz bead and one Pattern A bead set.

Beader's Tip *The length of thread you start with should be as long as you feel comfortable using. Some weavers can handle super-long threads, while others are a little more thread-challenged. To find out the best length for you, start with one yard (.9 m) and then work up from there, adding a little more thread until you find the length that you like best. This will be the length you should start with for most projects.*

18. String on one 4-mm light topaz crystal, one 4-mm olivine crystal, and one 4-mm light topaz crystal. From now on, this set of beads will be referred to as Pattern B.

19. Continue to string the following beads onto this same strand: one Pattern A, one 8-mm gold crystal, one Pattern A, and one Pattern B.

20. Repeat step 19 two times.

21. String one Pattern A, one 8-mm gold crystal, one Pattern A, and one 4-mm light topaz crystal.

21. Attach a **crimp bead** to the end of the beading wire, and slip on one **quadruple loop eye** before closing the crimp.

23. Repeat steps 17 through 22 for the other side of the strap, and attach the **triple loop hook** before closing the **crimp bead**.

Accents of red, pink, gray, and cream-colored seed beads are used to embroider around this triangular-shaped jasper cabochon. For the multiple-strand strap, the artist used an assortment of gemstone beads, including pearls, rhodonite, red goldstone, and faceted gray quartz.

Artist: Ruth Neese

Stitch Tip

*Unless you turn a beaded embroidery cabochon (on its edge), the sewn edging around it isn't noticeable. It's really up to you whether you prefer to cover the sides. However, if you prefer to cover the sides, **picot bead embroidery** is one option. Another alternative is to glue on decorative edges such as braid, lace, piping, or pre-strung beads around the finished cabochon.*

Luxuria Amulet

Luxurious shades of red, red, and more red beads make up this brilliant **chevron stitch** amulet necklace. The woven amulet has a textured appearance and is finished off with strand after strand of crystal and seed bead **basic fringe**. The strap is also loaded with sparkling beads and, as a bonus, the strap is detachable due to the **wrapped hooks**. Remove the strap from the **beaded loops** on either side of the amulet, flip it around, and connect the hooks to each other behind your neck for a 24-inch (61 cm) necklace. You'll feel like royalty whether you wear the necklace solo or with the entire amulet ensemble.

MATERIALS

- 15 grams ½" (1.3 cm) red silver-lined bugle beads

- 15 grams size 11 opaque cherry red Japanese seed beads

- twenty-five 4-mm red transparent matte square Japanese seed beads

- twenty-four 10 x 8-mm red AB teardrop crystal beads

- sixteen 6-mm red AB square crystal beads

- two 2 x 2-mm sterling silver crimp beads

- two sterling silver wrapped hooks (page 29)

- 3' (.9 m) size .014 beading wire

- Nymo thread, size B, in red

- beeswax or Thread Heaven

- size 12 beading needle

- scissors

- crimping pliers

1. **Condition** the Nymo thread, and the needle, using the **ladder stitch**, connect 40 bugle beads.

2. When you have reached the end of the ladder piece, use the same **ladder stitch** technique to connect the last bugle bead to the first one, thus making a circular ladder of beads.

3. Make three more ladder circles, using 40 bugle beads in each, for a total of four ladder sections.

4. Take two of the ladder sections just made, and follow steps 1 through 9 from the **chevron stitch** instructions to make a single chevron layer, using opaque cherry red seed beads to attach both ladder sections together.

5. Continue to use the **chevron stitch** and cherry red seed beads until all four ladder sections are connected. The result will be a tube of beads.

6. Select one end of the tube and, while holding both sides of the tube together, use a **whipstitch** to attach them. You have now made a basic amulet and are ready to embellish it with a strap and some fringe.

7. Determine which side you want to be the front of the amulet, and use the **adding thread** technique so that you have a piece of thread coming out of one end of a ladder rung on the front side.

8. Next, it's time to add ten strands of fringe. Use the **basic fringe** instructions, except instead of going back up through the same bugle bead in the ladder, insert the needle up through the bottom of the next bugle bead over in the ladder piece. Then bring the needle down through the bugle bead next to this one for the next strand of fringe (for the first strand of fringe, this will be the third bugle bead from the end), and continue this for all ten strands.

9. For the first strand of fringe, use the following bead pattern: four seed beads, one 4-mm cube bead, four seed beads, one teardrop bead (with the narrow end pointing toward the amulet for each fringe strand), and one seed bead.

10. For the second strand of fringe, use the following bead pattern: six seed beads, one 4-mm cube bead, six seed beads, one teardrop bead, and one seed bead.

11. For the third strand of fringe, use the following bead pattern: eight seed beads, one 4-mm cube bead, eight seed beads, one teardrop bead, and one seed bead.

12. For the fourth strand of fringe, use the following bead pattern: 10 seed beads, one 4-mm cube bead, 10 seed beads, one teardrop bead, and one seed bead.

13. For the fifth strand of fringe, use the following bead pattern: 12 seed beads, one 4-mm cube bead, 12 seed beads, one teardrop bead, and one seed bead.

14. Repeat step 13 for the sixth strand; step 12 for the seventh strand; step 11 for the eighth strand; step 10 for the ninth strand; and step 9 for the tenth strand of fringe, and use the **finishing thread** technique before continuing.

15. With a freshly threaded needle, use the **adding thread** technique and position the thread so that it is coming out of an end bugle bead at the top of the amulet.

16. Use the **Comanche stitch** and seed beads to embellish around the top of the amulet, making only one row of **Comanche**.

17. Attach **beaded loops**, each made up of ten seed beads, to either side of the amulet, and use the **finishing thread** technique.

18. Now it's time to make the strap. Add twelve seed beads and one **crimp bead** onto one end of the beading wire. Slip on the loop of one **wrapped hook** component, bring the end of the beading wire back through the **crimp bead** to form a loop of beads around the hook. Close the **crimp bead** with crimping pliers, and use wire cutters to trim off the excess beading wire.

19. String on one 6-mm crystal cube, five seed beads, one 4-mm cube, five seed beads, one 6-mm crystal cube, and five more seed beads.

20. Next, string on one teardrop bead (with the narrow end facing away from the beads previously strung), three seed beads, one 4-mm cube, and one teardrop bead (with the narrow end facing toward the beads previously strung).

21. Alternate steps 19 and 20, repeating step 19 seven more times and step 20 six more times.

22. Repeat step 18 to create a crimped beaded loop and hook on the other end, and slip both hooks around the beaded loops of the amulet to connect the strap.

This amulet is constructed of seed beads, rose quartz gemstones, and crystals in creams and pinks. The basic fringe embellishing the double chevron–patterned amulet is in graduated lengths. Wire-wrapped sterling hooks allow the wearer to remove the strap and wear it separately as a long necklace.

Artist: Tammy Powley

Double Chevron Bracelet

Between the two layers of **chevron stitch**. Connecting two beaded **ladder stitch** pieces, and the use of earth-tone Czech seed beads, you'll find it difficult to keep your hands off this heavily textured bracelet. Admirers will also want to touch it, and maybe even steal this right off your wrist if you aren't careful.

Earthy metal-colored beads and dark red seed beads are accented with two garnet stone beads for this rich **beaded toggle** bracelet. It looks intricate, but it's really not that difficult to make this bracelet, whose finished length is approximately 7 3/4 inches (19.7 cm).

MATERIALS

- 10 grams iris metallic bronze Czech seed beads

- 10 grams metallic silver Czech seed beads

- 10 grams opaque maroon Czech seed beads

- two 6-mm garnet beads

- Silamide thread in gold

- size 12 beading needle

- scissors

1. First, make two beaded **ladder stitch** sections using three bronze seed beads for each rung of the ladder. Both ladder sections should have a total of seventy-eight rungs each.

2. Use the **finishing thread** technique, and then continue with a freshly threaded needle.

3. Next, connect both ladder pieces together as described in steps 1 through 9 of the **chevron stitch** instructions, stringing on the first group of beads in the following order: one silver, one bronze, one maroon, one bronze, and one silver.

4. Bring the needle back through the last silver bead, which is the anchor bead as described in the **chevron stitch** instructions, and continue to thread on beads in this order: one bronze, one maroon, one bronze, and one silver. The last silver bead will continue to work as the anchor bead while you weave back and forth between the two ladder sections.

5. After connecting both ladder pieces and reaching the end, position the needle so that it is coming out of the middle of the **chevron stitch** area, and string on one 6-mm garnet bead.

6. Now string on fifteen bronze seed beads, and create the loop part of the **beaded toggle**. (Note: Because seed beads can vary in size, it's always a good idea to double-check that the beaded loop on a toggle fits around the other beaded end before finishing.)

7. At this point, you may need to use the **finishing thread** and **adding thread** techniques to start with a fresh piece of thread.

8. Following steps 10 and 11 from the **chevron stitch** instructions, weave back down the bracelet to create another row of **chevron stitch** on top of the first row.

9. At the end of the bracelet, use four bronze seed beads, one 6-mm garnet bead, and one bronze seed bead to make the other end of **the beaded toggle**, and **finish off** any existing threads.

Beader's Tip *If you decide to use beads whose dye or finish might wear off, such as galvanized or metal seed beads, think about how you plan to incorporate these into the design before you get started. A few of these beads used as accents may not lose their finish as quickly as those on a large beadwork piece that uses them as the primary bead. Experiment with fixatives, such as those manufactured by Krylon, to determine which products work best for your needs. Many craft stores and beading suppliers carry fixative products and may be able to recommend other brands for you to consider.*

Invariably, once you start making beautiful seed bead jewelry, family, friends, and even complete strangers will start to notice. Some may even ask to purchase your jewelry. Bead weaving can be very time-consuming, so once you get comfortable with a few stitches and techniques, it is a good idea to keep track of how much time it takes to make your most popular pieces. That way, if you ever decide to sell some of your work, you'll know how much time went into a piece, and how much you will want to charge for it.

A metal triangular toggle clasp accents the ends of this double chevron stitch bracelet, woven in sherbet-colored Czech seed beads. The matching Comanche stitch earrings include mother-of-pearl dangles on the ends of the fringe.

Artist: Cheri Auerbach

Woven Garnet Bracelet

Two needles are better than one. At least, that seems to be the case with this **double needle weave** garnet and copper-colored seed bead bracelet. The dark bohemian burgundy of the garnet gemstone beads are framed by twinkling bronze triangle-shaped Czech seed beads. **Bead tips** supply weavers with a convenient way to work with more than one thread at a time. A gold-filled lobster claw clasp and **jump ring** provide security while still letting you fasten it to your wrist easily. The finished length of this bracelet is 7 ½ inches (19.1 cm). To adjust the length, add or remove beads as necessary when weaving, allowing approximately 1 inch (2.5 cm) for the clasp. After making one of these bracelets in garnet and bronze, try other bead combinations so you'll have multiple wardrobe options.

MATERIALS

- 10 grams triangular bronze Czech seed beads

- sixty-two 4-mm garnet beads

- two size 11 round seed beads (any color)

- two gold-filled bead tips

- two 4-mm gold-filled jump rings (page 27)

- one 12-mm gold-filled lobster claw clasp

- Silamide thread in brown

- two size 12 beading needles

- scissors

- jeweler's cement

- flat-nosed pliers

- corsage pin or beading awl

- round-nosed pliers

1. After threading both needles, tie both ends of the threads together with an overhand knot. Use the jeweler's cement, flat-nosed pliers, corsage pin, and one size 11 round seed bead to attach one **bead tip** to the end of the threads.

2. String one bronze seed bead, one garnet bead, and two bronze seed beads onto the right thread.

3. String on one bronze seed bead, one garnet bead, and one bronze seed bead onto the left thread.

4. Now follow the **double needle weave** instructions to create the first stitch.

5. Repeat steps 2 through 4 until you have used all the garnet beads and finish (just like you started) with a bronze seed bead on each thread.

6. Finish the ends with another **bead tip** with a round seed bead inside, and then use round-nosed pliers to curl the hook on one **bead tip** around a **jump ring**.

7. Attach a **jump ring** to the lobster claw clasp, and then repeat step 6 to attach this to the other **bead tip**.

Stitch Tip

When looking for gemstone beads to incorporate into bead weaving stitches, take a good look at the beads' holes. Their size can vary depending on the quality and diameter of the bead, though 4 mm usually works well with many stitches. Some stitches require multiple passes with a needle and thread. If the holes are not large enough, then there is the option of using thinner needles and thinner thread, but these types of decisions are necessary before selecting beads for a particular stitch. Also, check around the edges of gemstone bead holes to make sure there are no cracks in the beads. This could later harm the integrity of the finished piece because the cracks could cause the beads to break.

Extra large beads may be too heavy for a regular seed bead stringing medium, such as Nymo or Silamide thread. One way around this is to try doubling the thread; however, there are lots of other threads that can be used for weaving, including beading wire, which is made up of multiple wire pieces that are entwined and coated. Beading wire comes in sizes as small as .010 mm in diameter. Some weavers attach needles to beading wire, but because the wire is stiff it can also act as a needle, allowing you to pierce seed bead holes easily.

Double needle weave is used for these beaded dangle earrings. The pearl earrings include sterling silver ear hooks with cube-shaped Pacific opal crystals. Czech crystals in light blue are woven with white seed beads for a second pair. The amber-colored crystals and bronze-colored Czech seed beads in the third pair have smoky quartz briolette dangles from the center and gold vermeil beads on the ear hooks.

Artist: Tammy Powley

Sparkling Spiral Bracelet

The **Dutch spiral** stitch instructions explain how to use five different types of beads for this stitch; however, you can use more or fewer than five, and the process is basically the same. For this bracelet, you will use four types of beads: freshwater pearls, amethyst gemstones, Czech crystals, and Japanese seed beads. This spiral of beads turns and twists, ending with a potato pearl **beaded toggle** clasp. The finished length of this bracelet, including the toggle, is about 8 inches

(20.3 cm), though, it will fit the average 7 to 7 ½-inch (17.8 cm to 19.1 cm) wrist. More length is necessary for this bracelet due to its diameter, which is roughly ½" (1.3 cm). Although pearls and amethysts work well together in this design, these types of beads often have irregular-shaped or extra-small holes, so make sure you have some extra beads of each type on hand in case you can't use some of them.

MATERIALS

- seventy-two 4-mm amethyst gemstone beads

- seventy-two 4-mm dark amethyst Czech crystals

- seventy-three 3- to 4-mm freshwater rice-shaped pearls

- 30 grams size 11 translucent rainbow dark amethyst Japanese seed beads

- one 6-mm potato-shaped pearl bead

- Silamide thread in lilac

- size 12 beading needle

- scissors

1. Start the **Dutch spiral stitch**, assigning the following letters to each bead: (A) amethyst gemstone beads, (B) crystal beads, and (C) freshwater pearls.

2. Because there are four types of beads in this bracelet rather than five, there will be no "D" bead assigned. Instead, assign the letter "E" to the seed beads.

3. Begin making a bead tube using the **Dutch spiral stitch** instructions, remembering to ignore any reference to the "D" bead, and leave an extra-long tail about 12" (30.5 cm) in length.

4. Continue weaving with the **Dutch spiral stitch** and the four different types of beads until the bead tube is about 7" (17.8 cm) in length.

5. String on five seed beads, one potato pearl, and one seed bead.

6. Then follow the **beaded toggle** instructions to make the pearl end of the toggle clasp, and **finish off** the working thread.

7. Attach the needle to the tail left in step 3, and string on enough seed beads to create a loop that will fit around the potato pearl. You'll need approximately fourteen seed beads, but the number can vary because both the seed beads and the pearls are not always uniform in size.

8. Follow the **beaded toggle** instructions to make the loop end of the toggle clasp, and double-check that the loop fits around the pearl before you **finish off** the thread.

Beader's Tip

Purchasing beads in different shades of the same color is a good way to build up a bead inventory. This will later provide "no-brainer" bead combinations for just about any beaded jewelry project. Many crystal beads come in dark and light shades and also duplicate some of the more popular gemstone colors, such as amethyst, garnet, and rose quartz. Gemstones originally come from nature rather than a manufacturer, so their depth of color can vary a great deal. Many stone beads are color-treated, either through heating or dying; this can also make a significant color difference.

Cyndy Klein gives the Dutch spiral stitch a new twist by combining seed beads and crystals for these dazzling earrings, which the artist calls Crystal Twist. Brightly colored Austrian crystals and seed beads make up the spiral. By inserting a head pin through the bead base, Cyndy creates a way to attach an ear hook to the top and a crystal dangle to the bottom of each earring.

Artist: Cyndy Klein

Howlite Spiral Necklace

A **Dutch spiral** woven tube of beads is the centerpiece of this 24" (61 cm) necklace. Shades of blue, ranging from rich royal blue to sky blue, are highlighted with howlite gemstone beads, which have gray streaks throughout. By attaching bead strands, which are 8½" (21.6 cm) long on each side, to the 6-inch (15.2 cm) beaded spiral, more length is added without spending the extra time to make a necklace-length spiral. The addition of a necklace strap is also a nice way to add even more unique bead styles to the piece. A gold-filled **quadruple loop eye** and a **triple loop hook** are attached to **bead tips** to complete the design.

MATERIALS

- eighty 4-mm light sapphire–colored Czech crystal beads

- sixty-two 4-mm howlite beads

- fifty-six 4-mm royal blue square Czech seed beads

- fifty-six size 6 matte cobalt blue Czech seed beads

- 30 grams size 11 rainbow light blue Japanese seed beads

- twelve 10 x 8-mm cobalt blue teardrop Czech crystal beads

- six 8-mm howlite beads

- two gold-filled bead tips

- one gold-filled quadruple loop eye (page 30)

- one gold-filled triple loop hook (page 30)

- Silamide thread in royal blue

- size 12 beading needle

- scissors

- jeweler's cement

- flat-nosed pliers

- corsage pin or beading awl

- round-nosed pliers

1. Start the **Dutch spiral stitch**, assigning the following letters to each of the five types of beads: (A) light sapphire-colored crystal beads, (B) 4-mm howlite beads, (C) square beads, (D) matte cobalt blue beads, (E) size 11 seed beads.

2. Begin making a bead tube using the **Dutch spiral stitch** instructions, and leave about a 6" (15.2 cm) thread tail.

3. Continue weaving with the **Dutch spiral stitch** and the five different types of beads until the bead tube is about 6"(15.2 cm) in length.

4. Use the **finishing thread** technique to finish off the tail and working thread.

5. Rethread the needle with about 30"(76.2 cm) of thread, pull the thread so that it is a double thickness, and use the **adding thread** technique to attach the end of the doubled thread to one end of the beaded tube completed in step 4.

6. String on one teardrop bead (narrow end pointing away from the bead tube), one seed bead, one 4-mm light sapphire-colored crystal, one seed bead, one 4-mm howlite bead, one seed bead, one 4-mm light sapphire-colored crystal, one seed bead, and one teardrop bead (narrow end pointing toward the beads previously strung). This is now referred to as Pattern A.

7. String on five size 11 seed beads.

8. String on one 4-mm light sapphire-colored crystal, one 8-mm howlite bead, and one 4-mm light sapphire-colored crystal. This is now referred to as Pattern B.

9. String on five size 11 seed beads, one Pattern A, five size 11 seed beads, and one Pattern B.

10. Repeat step 9, and then use the jeweler's cement, flat-nosed pliers, and corsage pin to finish the end with a **bead tip**.

11. Repeat steps 5 through 10 for the other side of the necklace strap.

12. Use round-nosed pliers to curl the hook on one **bead tip** around a **quadruple loop eye**, and then repeat this to attach the **triple loop hook** to the other **bead tip**.

Stitch Tip

*When working through the **Dutch spiral stitch**, it can sometimes get confusing about which bead to insert your needle through. Once you get it started, however, you'll soon notice that you will go through the same bead that you just strung onto the thread. Therefore, if you string on a howlite bead, then that means you insert the needle through the next howlite bead on the spiral. If you string on a blue crystal, then that means you insert the needle through the next blue crystal bead on the spiral, and so on.*

Beader's Tip *Beaded necklace straps are normally made up of two strands of beads to attach amulets, beaded cabochons, and other woven designs to the wearer's neck. When stringing up symmetrical necklace straps, always take a few moments while working to ensure that your chosen bead pattern is correct and you haven't accidentally left out a bead or put beads in the wrong order. Then after stringing the second strap, make sure both straps match before finishing. Just a few extra minutes spent double-checking will save you from having to restring designs due to simple errors.*

In this piece, the artist uses her Curling Fantasy Tube design technique in a different color palette, this time primarily in shades of gold. The necklace is sculpted around a large lampwork bead created by Tom Boylan. Both necklaces include a hook-and-eye clasp.

Artist: Lisa Niven Kelly

Beaded Bead Bracelet

You can make your own beads from beads, and then intersperse them with peach aventurine gemstone beads and ethnic sterling silver beads for this cool, sherbet-colored bracelet. Perfect for practicing **even count flat peyote** or learning this stitch for the first time, these bracelets, constructed of woven Delica seed beads, are super easy to make. Plus, you get the added benefit of proclaiming that you actually made some of the beads in this design. The finished beads are shaped like tubes, so they thread easily onto beading wire. Complete the bracelet with **crimp beads** and a chunky sterling silver toggle clasp.

MATERIALS

- 10 grams lined lemon/lime Delica beads

- 10 grams lined purple/salmon Delica beads

- nine 6-mm peach aventurine beads

- twelve 4-mm clear AB bicone Swarovski crystal beads

- six 6-mm Bali-style sterling silver bead caps

- eight 6-mm sterling silver daisy spacer beads

- two 2 x 2-mm sterling silver tube crimp beads

- one 12-mm Bali-style sterling silver toggle clasp

- 12" (30.5 cm) size .014-mm beading wire

- Silamide thread in off-white

- size 12 beading needle

- scissors

- crimping pliers

- wire cutters

1. Start by making the beaded beads from both colors of Delica beads. After threading the needle, add a **stop bead**, and string on six lemon/lime Delicas.

2. Using the **even count flat peyote stitch**, weave ten rows of lemon/lime Delicas to form a square. (To double-check that you have the correct number of rows, count the beads on either side of the square. You should have five on one side and five on the other for a total of ten rows.)

3. Fold the beaded square in half. Hold the sides up next to each other, and lock the beads together (they look like little teeth).

4. Continue to hold the beaded peyote piece, locking the beads together, and insert the needle up through the bottom of the bead closest to the needle.

5. Connect both sides by threading the needle up through the teeth (the beads sticking out) so you zigzag back and forth.

6. Repeat the zigzag stitching back down in the opposite direction, **finish off** all threads, and remove the **stop bead**.

7. Repeat steps 1 through 6 until you have made four beaded beads, two with lemon/lime Delicas and two with purple/salmon Delicas. Set these aside for later use.

8. Finish the end with a **crimp bead**, making sure to add on one side of the toggle clasp before closing the **crimp bead** with crimping pliers.

9. String on beads in the following order: bead cap, aventurine bead, bead cap, crystal bead, aventurine bead, crystal bead, daisy spacer, lemon/lime beaded bead, daisy spacer, crystal bead, aventurine bead, crystal bead, daisy spacer, purple/salmon beaded bead, daisy spacer, crystal bead, aventurine bead, and crystal bead.

10. Repeat step 9, and then string on one bead cap, one aventurine bead, and another bead cap to complete the strung beads.

11. Finish the end with a **crimp bead**, making sure to add on the other end of the toggle clasp before closing the **crimp bead** with crimping pliers.

Stitch Tip

*Sometimes it can be helpful when learning a stitch for the first time, especially with a stitch such as **even count flat peyote**, to use two different colors of seed beads and to alternately string them on as you weave. The alternating colors will give you a better understanding of the weaving pattern as you become familiar with the new stitch. Alternating bead colors can create an interesting pattern as well.*

Ruby Fischer used the peyote stitch (one of her favorites) to weave this bracelet with size 8 bronze hex-cut beads and size 11 seed beads. The center embellishment is a faux pearl, and both the pearl and the edges of the bracelet are accented with a picot stitch variation. A beaded toggle finishes the design.

Artist: Ruby Fischer

Pearl Double Needle Necklace

Because of advanced techniques in pearl farming, pearl jewelry has become an affordable luxury; a democratized adornment for the masses. Luxurious is the perfect word to describe the feel of this woven pearl necklace, accented with turquoise-colored Japanese seed beads. Large 5-mm potato pearls, also referred to as semi-round, are an economical choice for this richly classic design. Once you finish crafting this necklace, you'll find that it somehow, almost instantly, appears around your neck. The finished length, including the sterling **quadruple loop eye** and **triple loop hook**, is approximately 16" (40.6 cm).

MATERIALS

- ❯ 10 grams size 11 luster light turquoise Japanese seed beads

- ❯ one hundred twenty-eight 5-mm potato-shaped pearls

- ❯ two sterling silver bead tips

- ❯ one sterling silver quadruple loop eye (page 30)

- ❯ one sterling silver triple loop hook (page 30)

- ❯ Nymo thread, size B, in turquoise

- ❯ beeswax or Thread Heaven

- ❯ two size 12 beading needles

- ❯ jeweler's cement

- ❯ flat-nosed pliers

- ❯ corsage pin or beading awl

- ❯ round-nosed pliers

- ❯ scissors

1. **Condition** two pieces of Nymo with beeswax, thread both needles, and tie both ends of the threads together with an overhand knot. Use the jeweler's cement, flat-nosed pliers, and corsage pin to attach one **bead tip** to the end of the threads.

2. String one seed bead, one pearl bead, and two seed beads onto the right-side thread.

3. String one seed bead, one pearl, and one seed bead onto the left-side thread.

4. Now follow the **double needle weave stitch** instructions to create the first stitch.

5. Repeat steps 2 through 4 until you have used all the pearl beads and finish (just like you started) with a seed bead on each thread.

6. Finish the ends with a **bead tip**, and then use round-nosed pliers to curl the hook on one **bead tip** around a **quadruple loop eye**.

7. Repeat step 6 to attach the **triple loop hook** to the other **bead tip**.

Beader's Tip

Most seed bead instructions will provide an approximate gram weight needed for seed beads rather than an exact count. Other than the fact that seed beads are normally sold by the gram, it is usually a good idea to have more than the minimum required seed beads for a project. Not all beads in a package may be useable. Even the occasional Japanese seed bead may have an odd shape and should be tossed. Also, beads this tiny can easily roll off a work surface and be lost among carpet fibers. It is better to have too many beads than not enough.

Stitch Tip

Products used for conditioning thread can eventually dry out. A little goes a long way, so you'll probably have that chunk of beeswax or little blue box of Thread Heaven around for a while. To help keep them from drying out too quickly, keep these items in a plastic bag or an airtight container. Also be careful where you store them. A traveling bead box filled with beading supplies left in a hot car can become a box full of melted beeswax in a relatively short period of time.

CHAPTER FOUR
GALLERY OF JEWELRY

Cheri Auerbach

Sumptuous vintage crystals glow in this heavily fringed amulet. A cascade of glass flower and leaf beads is woven across the front of the pink and green netting. The detachable strap is strung on beading wire and includes more vintage crystals and bead caps.

Right: Here, the artist used netting to encase a large metal bead for this necklace's focal point. Basic fringe trimmings dangle from the center with blue sodalite stars and bright blue and silver vintage crystals. The strap also includes stars and sparkling blue crystals.

In this piece, the artist wove around a tiny aromatherapy bottle using the netting stitch, then attached a strap of amber-colored glass, crystals, and black seed beads. The bottom of the bottle is embellished with more crystals and seed beads using the basic fringe technique.

Right: The artist designed and constructed this netted fused-glass cabochon necklace. The strap of this piece incorporates red and white seed beads woven with the chevron stitch. Luscious amounts of fringe include an assortment of mother-of-pearl hearts and square beads, along with red glass hearts, birds, and rectangular beads.

Joanne Strehle Bast

www.jbast.com

This turquoise gemstone necklace and earring set takes peyote stitch to a new level. On the necklace, the artist first wove turquoise chips into the peyote stitching and then attached a Czech lampworked glass pendant using a peyote-stitched loop, which is also textured with bead embroidery on the surface. The necklace straps are also peyote stitched, but Joanne made multiple peyote strips and then braided them together. Accompanying the necklace are matching earrings that incorporate ceramic horses hand-sculpted by Cindy Meyer.

Rhona Farber

Over the Moon Jewelry, www.overthemoonjewelry.com

This metallic-finished necklace and earring set combines like-colored seed beads, bugle beads, and freshwater pearls. The artist used single thread netting stitch for the necklace, with stations and dangles accented by pearls. For the earrings, Rhona combined the ladder stitch, Comanche stitch, and basic fringe technique.

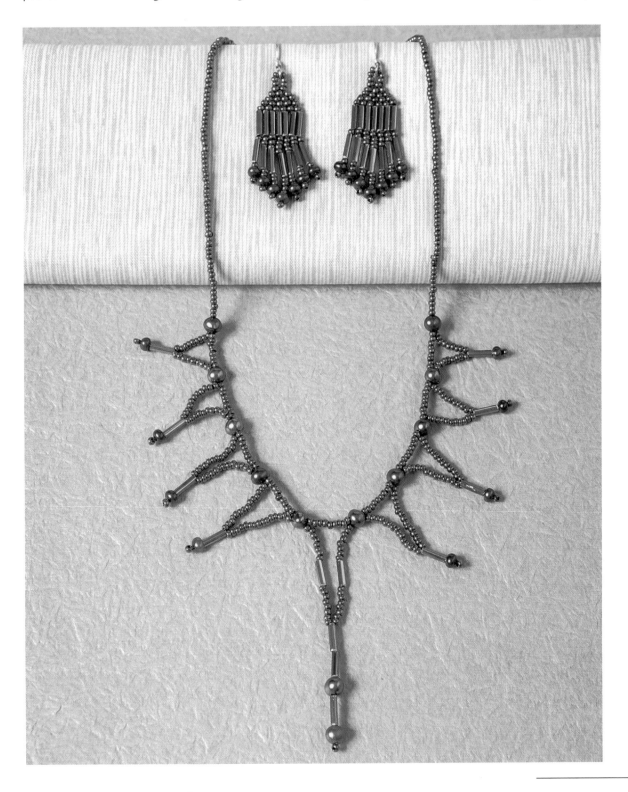

Ruby Fischer

Ruby's Beadwork, www.rubysbeadwork.com

Right: Bronze-colored pearls accent the strap as well as the center of this necklace. Chevron stitch becomes upscale couture with these silver-lined brown aurora borealis seed beads.

Below: This hefty peyote bracelet is made of beautiful nickel seed beads and embellished with glass turquoise-colored cabochons. The artist's choice of beads provides both a visual and a kinesthetic appeal to the finished piece.

Iris purple size 8 hex-cut beads and silver-lined teal seed beads combine in this peyote stitched bracelet. The placement of the teal and purple beads creates a checkerboard design across the piece, which includes a beaded toggle clasp and picot stitch edging. In the second peyote and toggle bracelet, she combined an unusual spectrum of colors in similar shades of purple including 4-mm purple-shaped beads and silver-lined purple seed beads.

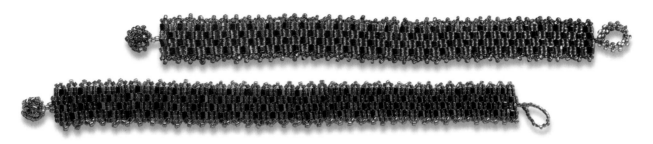

Lisa Niven Kelly

Leela Beads, www.leelabeads.com

Bead weaving can even be used to craft rings. Lisa calls these Queen's Rings. She made the coiled sterling silver tubes from fine-gauge wire using a technique similar to that of making jump rings. Then she stitched the coils together using the ladder stitch. The edges are finished with a picot-type embellishment of crystals and seed beads, and a Swarovski crystal rests in the center of each ring.

This necklace is called a Curling Fantasy Tube—its free-form sculptural peyote and netting stitch form a tube of beads. Lisa used different sizes of seed beads, in colors of red, gold, sliver, and blue to accent the focal lampwork bead created by Tom Boylan.

Jennifer Shibona

Right: Blue seed beads in various shades are highlighted in this hourglass-shaped bracelet with white seed beads and light and dark blue pearls. Each end of the bracelet, which closes with a double button toggle clasp, is stitched with Comanche, and the center strands meet together with the square stitch.

Below: Comanche stitch is allowed to express itself in this upside-down triangle with swag fringe. The fringe also includes 4-mm jet-black bicone crystals. The artist attached a pin finding to the back and covered it with black leather.

Right: A tubular style of the netting stitch is used for the strap on this dramatic necklace, finished off with a Bali-style S-hook clasp. The center was woven using Comanche stitch, combining bugle and round seed beads, and is embellished with basic fringe. Crystals dangle from the ends of the fringe.

Below: Variations of peyote stitching are used for this green and black bracelet. Even the ruffle center around the fused glass cabochon is peyote. The artist also added a spin to the basic beaded toggle for the bracelet's clasp.

Laurie Wedge

Lillypad Jewelry, www.lilypadjewelry.com

The artist adds a bit of whimsy to a free-form sculptural peyote bracelet. Using a variety of sizes of seed beads in tan, blue, and greens, she found inspiration in nature with the addition of a silver lizard button clasp.

Shiho Yamashita

www.shihoyamashita.com

By combining Japanese weaving techniques with traditional stitches, such as double needle weave, this artist and teacher creates a signature look. These intricate pieces are strung with fine beading wire instead of Nymo or Silamide. The bracelet is made from mother-of-pearl and seed beads and includes a beaded toggle clasp. The ring is also made of mother-of-pearl and seed beads.

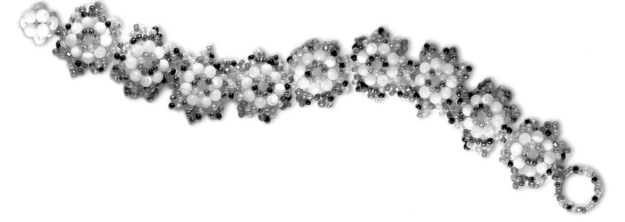

Artgems Inc.com
Phone: 480.545.6009
Website: www.artgemsinc.com

Auntie's Beads
Phone: 866.26.BEADS
Website: www.auntiesbeads.com

Beadalon
Phone: 866.423.2325
Website: www.beadalon.com

The Bead Warehouse
Phone: 301.565.0487
Website: www.thebeadwarehouse.com

B'Sue Boutiques
Website: www.bsueboutiques.com

CGM
Phone: 800.426.5246
Website: www.cgmfindings.com

Copper Coyote
Phone: 520.722.8440
Website: www.coppercoyote.com

Gemshow Online Jewelry Supply
Phone: 877.805.7440
Website: www.gemshow-online.com

HHH Enterprises
Phone: 800.777.0218
Website: www.hhhenterprises.com

Land of Odds
Phone: 615.292.0610
Website: www.landofodds.com

Monsterslayer
Phone: 505.598.5322
Website: www.monsterslayer.com

Out on a Whim
Phone: 800.232.3111
Website: www.whimbeads.com

Rings and Things
Phone: 800.366.2156
Website: www.rings-things.com

Rio Grande
Phone: 800.545.6566
Website: www.riogrande.com

Shipwreck Beads
Phone: 800.950.4232
Website: www.shipwreck-beads.com

Soft Flex Company
Phone: 707.938.3539
Website: www.softflextm.com

South Pacific Wholesale Co.
Phone: 800.338.2162
Website: www.beading.com

Wire-Sculpture.com
Phone: 877.636.0600
Website: www.wire-sculpture.com

INTERNATIONAL

African Trade Beads
Website: www.africantradebeads.com

The Bead Company of Australia
Phone: 02.9281.7111
Website: www.beadcompany.com.au

Beadfx
Phone: 877.473.2323
Website: www.beadfx.com

Beadgems
Phone: 0845.123.2743
Website: www.beadgems.com

The Bead Shop
Phone: 0127.374.0777
Website: www.beadsunlimited.co.uk

Beadworks
Phone: 0207.240.0931
Website: www.beadshop.co.uk

Canadian Beading Supply
Phone: 800.291.6668
Website: www.canbead.com

Gem Craft
Phone: 0161.477.0435
Website: www.gemcraft.co.uk

Hobbycraft
Stores throughout the United Kingdom
Phone: 0120.259.6100

The House of Orange
Phone: 250.483.1468
Website: www.houseoforange.biz

Katie's Treasures
Phone: 02.4956.3435
Website: www.katiestreasures.com.au

Kernowcrafts Rocks and Gems Limited
Phone: 0187.257.3888
Website: www.kernowcraft.com

Mee Ngai Wah in Sham Shui Po
Tel: 8171.3226
Fax: 8171.3312

Spacetrader Beads
Phone: 03.9534.6867
Website: www.spacetrader.com.au

SUPPLIERS

The following companies generously donated the supplies used for creating the jewelry projects in this book:

Beadshop.com
158 University Avenue
Palo Alto, CA 94301
USA
Phone: 650.328.5291
Email: webmanager@beadshop.com
Website: www.beadshop.com

Beadshop.com is the website of The Bead Shop, which also has a storefront in Palo Alto, California. They offer a large selection of exceptional quality beads, findings, and tools. In addition to selling supplies, the talented team of in-house designers make their own jewelry kits; distribute multimedia classes through DVD, CD, video, and downloadable project instructions; and also provide on-site classes in a wide variety of jewelry techniques from metalsmithing to beading.

Fire Mountain Gems and Beads
One Fire Mountain Way
Grants Pass, OR 37526-2373
USA
Phone: 800.423.2319
Website: www.firemountaingems.com

Fire Mountain Gems and Beads has just about everything a jewelry maker needs, including beads, wire, tools, books, and other related jewelry products. Shop with them online or browse through their full-color catalog available both on CD and in hard copy. Along with lots of wonderful jewelry supplies, their catalog and website offers free tips and project ideas. Their 800-number is manned 24 hours a day, and you can call toll-free from anywhere in the U.S. or Canada.

ABOUT THE AUTHOR

Tammy Powley is a writer and designer. She is the author of two jewelry books, *Making Designer Gemstone and Pearl Jewelry* and *Making Designer Bead and Wire Jewelry*. Besides print publications, Tammy is the Internet guide for About.com's jewelry-making website at http://jewelrymaking.about.com, keeps a beading and jewelry blog at www.aboutweblogs.com/jewelrybeading/, and operates her own website at www.tammypowley.com. Tammy has studied a wide variety of jewelry techniques, from beading to metalsmithing and has worked extensively with glass, fibers, and paper art. After spending eight years on the art show circuit, she eventually turned to writing about art, though she continues to sell her work through special commissions. Tammy currently resides in Port St. Lucie, Florida, with her husband, Michael, and a house full of dogs and cats.

ACKNOWLEDGMENTS

I want to give a big thank you and a hug to each of my local seed bead buddies: Cheri Auerbach, Ruth Neese, and Jennifer Shibona. Without these three friends, who helped me learn many of the stitches in this book, answered my constant questions, shared their tips and expertise, and quieted my doubts while designing projects, I never would have managed.

Thank you to my editor, Mary Ann Hall, and the other talented individuals at Quarry who worked together on this project. Their attention to detail and dedication to producing a quality product is outstanding.

Judy Love is an amazing illustrator who doesn't mind picking up a needle, thread, and some beads to make sure a stitch is presented clearly and correctly. I feel blessed to have had another opportunity to work with her.

I'm also very grateful to the suppliers who donated many of the beads and supplies for this book. Beadshop.com and Fire Mountain Gems and Beads have been very generous. The supplies they donated to assist with projects and photographs were tremendously helpful. Their quality products gave me inspiration to create quality projects.

I'm in debt to all of the artists who contributed their beautiful bead work to the gallery and variation projects. Their combined talents are awesome! They really came through for me and helped create a wonderful addition to this book. Seeing all the different approaches to similar stitches and techniques was a big treat.

Finally, of course, thank you to my husband, Michael, who is always supportive. No matter how many projects I'm juggling, he keeps me grounded.